EXMOOR AMOUR

For Joy and Maurice

EXMOOR
AmouR

CHARLES WOOD

HALSGROVE

First published in Great Britain in 2010

Illustrated by the author

Also by Charles Wood:
How to Survive in Somerset
Suriving Another Somerset Year
Charles Wood's Somerset Quiz Book

Publisher's Disclaimer
As is well known, Halsgrove have disowned Mr Wood on many occasions
in the past and this particular volume is no exception. The views expressed
herein arise entirely from the fevered brain of Mr Wood who remains
entirely responsible for them, the Publisher is pleased to say.

British Library Cataloguing-in-Publication Data
A CIP record for this title is available from the British Library

ISBN 978 0 85704 048 0

HALSGROVE
Halsgrove House,
Ryelands Industrial Estate,
Bagley Road, Wellington, Somerset TA21 9PZ
Tel: 01823 653777   Fax: 01823 216796
email: sales@halsgrove.com

Part of the Halsgrove group of companies
Information on all Halsgrove titles is available at: www.halsgrove.com

Printed and bound by Short Run Press Ltd., Exeter

Naming of Parts

Acknowledgements

Over the years Exmoor has been most kind to both me and my tummy. So first and foremost my extended thanks to her are my priority. For giving purpose to my ramblings over the past year, and for his confidence in me to not let the side down too much, I extend gratitude to Steven Pugsley at Halsgrove.

However, without the rich contributions of friends this book would have been rather self-opinionated. Therefore humungus gratitude must go to Gill and Jeremy, Mark and Fiona, Phil, Joan, Patrick and Ray for their unceasing enlightenment of all things wonderful.

To Romi and Mona who provided me with their warmth of hospitality and lessons in making sarmale with dextrous fingers from rolled cabbage leaves, my thanks are profound.

Closer to home I can only give my heartfelt gratitude to my wife for her love and for unceasingly encouraging my pastime of keypad tapping.

And a mention for Bilbo, my reliable early morning alarm, for raising the author from his duvet warmth to become more productive with the day.

ONE

Rat, Rabbit and Rag

*"The sea helps in fixing the boundaries of what we may call the area under
Exmoor influence, or the Exmoor region. The long arm of the Bristol Channel
clearly marks the north of the region. Along the coast the limits with which
we need concern ourselves are Combe Martin in the West, where the River
Umber finds the sea; and in the east Watchet, close to Blue Anchor and all that
now remains of the once glorious abbey of Cleeve.*

*From Watchet a fairly eastern boundary suggests itself: south along the B3190
to the BBC Station at Washford Cross; thence to Fair Cross and so along
B3188 to Monksilver, Elsworthy, close to Brompton Ralph and on to Wiveliscombe. That, I think, gives us our eastern boundary."*

Lawrence Meynell, *Exmoor* 1953.

Sometimes it's only when a west country chap is far, far away from what
he takes for granted, like a Porlock Bay dogfish under the kitchen fillet
knife, that he realises what he's missing. And I really was a very long way
from the familiar.

Let me explain with an anecdote from a thick-wet autumnal day, much like
one that disgruntled Parliamentary Commissioners of the Cromwellian
lobster helmet era when in 1651 they described Exmoor as "a Mountenous
and cold ground much be Clouded with thick Foggs and Mists". The local
winding country lanes had lost their intimacy and become downright ruddy
dangerous. For all that I was able to see I could well have been catching a

chill upon Dunkery. But no, I wasn't. Instead, I was high in the wooded tea growing hills of Nilgiris in Southern India where the British had built their imperial hill-stations of Ooty and Conoor, enjoying a climate much like Stoke Pero but with an annual dragonfly migration, staggering in numbers. Here puffs a regular steam train reminiscent of any on the West Somerset Railway. While on the roads, danger comes not from meandering tractors but from careering tuk-tuks and rickety buses.

And on the subject of buses, I'd had visions the week before that I'd decided to put behind me. "Everybody's got to be somewhere!" Ahmednagar-born Spike Milligan shouted out during the last Goon Show, apparently from the depths of a coal cellar. Well, I was with my wife in the back of a struggling taxi on a narrow Indian road, stuck behind a packed gear-grinding bus. An unfortunate, leaning out the bus's rear window, chuddered endless streams that turned into brown pellets on hitting the road's warm surface. Some hit the taxi windscreen.

Turning my gaze for a change of scenery, my head suddenly made like a barn owl's. At the roadside was a vision from the past, one that had vanished off the radar almost two decades ago. A small, grey-bearded Eurasian bloke in a short-sleeved check shirt was helping a thin Indian man in shorts and flip-flops to move a nondescript skeletal and exhausted scabby dog to a van marked IAR – International Animal Rescue. At this point the taxi driver who saw an overtaking opportunity floored the accelerator pedal and my view became dust.

With a clear road ahead once more, I said to my wife, 'I knew that bearded chap, the one with the dog back there.'

"What man?' What dog? Is it safe to open my eyes?" she said.

"Hmm-hmm," I replied then, lost myself to memories of the late 1980s when I was a cameraman filming Exmoor hunting features for BBC Points West. The chap in question was undoubtedly John Hicks who had spoken frequently and animatedly into my lens about the blood lust delirium of hunters. He had but one mantra: "Hunting's barbaric, ban hunting". This confrontational field operative of the League Against Cruel Sports was a layer of false trails, the bane of the huntsman and a frustration to the athletic hound. Tirelessly antagonistic, he and his battered beige Subaru pick-up blaring out operatic arias were a regular arrival wherever the Devon and Somerset Staghounds had a meet, whether that was outside an Exmoor pub or in a farmyard. Oh boy, did he get folks' ganders up.

On studio playback my soundtracks took on a surreal quality, full of the toot of the hunting horn and *Madame Butterfly* as well as unprecedented blue language. John was driven by sheer cussed bloody-mindedness. Shrugging off adverse comments aimed at him, he was seemingly oblivious that his actions might untwine the traditions of rural life. Or, indeed, that his masters were urban politicos with personal agendas of Westminster opportunity. And it must have seemed quite perverse to John that the Chairman and Executive Director of the League Against Cruel Sports, Richard Course later reconsidered the League's standpoint with the immortal utterance: "the simple prohibition of staghunting would destroy the survival prospects of wild red deer in the West Country". Blooming marvellous.

However, with the damage done and with hounds and horses now having to chase rats, rabbits or scented rags instead of stags, I could never have imagined that John would have made a new life for himself being 'pelleted' beside an Indian road, while giving solace to a mutt incapable of chasing anything. But as I said, I'd put the visions behind myself.

Far better to think of the positives of home, like the *Voices of Exmoor* whose harmonies and camaraderie amongst the thirty-five singers was helping the UK charity 'Reaching the Unreached' raise money to set up support for orphans and poor local villagers in the countryside through which I was passing.

I chatted with Chaggi, a twenty-something cook from Rajasthan who liked to dance spontaneous Bollywood dervishly, whirling a tea towel. He had identified that I was from 'Great England' shortly after my arrival amid the annual migration of dragonfly millions when I let slip more than one or two 'oh, m'dears' as wing vibrations tickled my face.

Chaggi and I had quickly glossed past influence of my countrymen in these local parts and in the sub-continent generally.

"The English had been a bit naughty," I ventured.

"We were deluded," countered Chaggi.

Well, so was I. 'Relax! Revive!! Rejuvenate!!!' the webpage had said of Chaggi's workplace.

For his masala tea Chaggi had been milking a black and white cow like one of those so common in rural Blighty, only this one understood Hindi. And both he and I were taking a time-out. Mine was from a hard-core ayurvedic weight loss experience of yoga and scalding hot, medicinal herb-bag pummellings; ghee gulping and purgation; not to mention vegetarianism. Although I politely avoided Chaggi's curried beetroot, apparently good for constipation and haemorrhoids, cabbage, coming with coconut and thin rice soup, was fed to me daily. Too much cheddar, butter wedges on crusty white farmhouse bread and crispy Dunster free-range chicken skin had created me a girth in need of desperate measures.

A sparrow chirped forlornly looking every inch a dead-ringer for the many that daily visited the bird table in the narrow Wiveliscombe lane called 'Skoda Row', nicknamed such because of the number of four-wheeled Czech mates now owned by several householders and their neighbours who argued over parking space until the bim-boms and caterwauls called time. This was home - a small town that for ease of spelling became known simply as 'Wivey'.

Perhaps the Indian sparrow had become lonely. Out there in the murk I knew the local meat-eaters were nibbling. But for once I wasn't jealous. Sparrows in India are viewed as aphrodisiacs due to their public exhibitions of libido and as a consequence are becoming a somewhat rare treat. Yet, in a moment of herb-induced clarity, I comprehended why Bilbo, my patio-tree sentinel, aged, stripy cat, behaved like a tart.

And there were other tweaks of home. Twelve hours earlier, somewhere up north, Hyderabad I think, Somerset's cricketers had sung lustily about a blackbird in a wurzel tree and a great big stick to knock him down. It was the happiest moment of their captain Justin Langer's illustrious career. The team had beaten Deccan Chargers in a 20/20 game of bish-bash-bosh, earning the players enough to continue sipping their Starbucks coffee on their return to Taunton. I said as much to Chaggi.

"Marcus Trescothick," said Chaggi, "We love him here. But he should drink our black tea, it would help his stress.' Then with the ayurvedic wisdom added, 'Mr Trescothick must be told coffee's very bad. It makes the jingly-jangles."

"Perhaps they should start tea plantations on Exmoor," I mused. "The weather seems to be the same."

"Exmoor?" said Chaggi. "What's Exmoor?"

Well, that did it. Thinking of Britain's least-visited and most intimate national park made my emotion spring flow. It's the 'Ex' in Exmoor that makes things so disconcerting. I long ago ceased to refer to the place as 'it' but as 'her'. And now, like an old flame, memories of her burn happily long after separation. And then, occasionally, not so happily, like a summer fire that makes charcoal of heather and gorse. Such are the foibles of the heart – of amour. Sadly, it seems she exhibits her cleavage to all and sundry, or so a friend with geological bent told me. Something to do with rock layers. I closed my ears when he got onto the bit about 'bedding' and the earth moving.

In outline she's not very glamorous, looking more like a giant flat-splat turtle after a road kill attempt. Her head and high Dunkery shell lie in Somerset, while her nether regions flop into Devon, where rumours have it, one can discover Twitchen. But don't get your hopes up as it's just a derivation of 'twicene', the Old English for a fork in the road.

I spoke of red deer stags roaring louder than Bengal tigers and of venison sausages; of trout splashing beneath carnivorous midge clouds by fast flowing streams; of woods and waterfalls in steep ravines, of buzzards mewing in the fashion of new born kittens over whortleberry moorland; of the dismal whining of gulls above towering sea cliffs bearing weathered rock formations with names like *Ragged Jack* or *Mother Meldrum's Gut*; of grockles and locals alike playing Pooh-sticks with the nostalgia of 'cream tea England' from the delightful packhorse bridges at Allerford and Dunster; and of a very, very small place called Charles.

My voice trailed away as I daydreamed of a rare golden afternoon, long before my tummy took flight towards Chaggi's kitchen, when two of Dunkery's long-horned shaggy highland cattle parted car drivers of saga age like a biblical sea. A calf anxiously trotted in tow, possibly catching my thoughts of veal escalope with wild mushroom sauce.

My reverie was interrupted by a series of violent bangs. "Good God, Chaggi," I said, "This place actually sounds like Exmoor."

"Firecrackers. Ghandi's birthday. Hindu festival," informed Chaggi. "You celebrate Ghandi's birthday?"

"Nah, we just shoot pheasants…and the odd triangular metallic road sign." In truth this had been going on for aeons. But this was just a ballistics sideshow amid Exmoor's rich tapestry of life.

"On my return to Somerset, Chaggi, I vow to seek her out again; and, of course, reacquaint myself with the eclectic bundle of humanity who share her."

"Good thinkings," said Chaggi. "Your lady seems entertaining."

"Oh, she never ceases to amaze," I said, before worrying whether Chaggi and I were on the same wave-length; and about beetroot being the only item on that evening's menu.

Ayurveda Yoga Retreat, Conoor, Autumn 2009.

T W O

Tapping Sensibilities

"Some of us are like wheelbarrows - only useful when pushed, and very easily upset."

Jack Herbert

There is a little known but true story of a grey-haired artist who had shut up his house in Cornwall. With only £5 in his pocket and all his painting paraphernalia in a satchel he had set out to walk and paint his way through England, selling pictures as he went and living off the proceeds. When he reached Lynton, having walked eight hundred miles and painted and sold innumerable pictures, he was asked which part of all those miles he had found the most beautiful. His reply was unhesitating and consisted of one word – "Exmoor". I had travelled much further, albeit by plane, tuk-tuk, bus and car, and could only empathise with that artist.

A thinner me had returned home at the time of year when the red deer stags were exercising their vocal cords by bolving, days were falling in, and daddy-granfers had ensconced themselves in the damp dark of cottage squinches. Rumours had come, blown in with the draughts, of snow making machines, of water-spitting dinosaurs, of hovering helicopters and low-flying jets, of farmers having teddy troubles and of bibblers cuddling grouse. Apparently the 'Aksmoar' weasel patrols were proving alarmingly ineffective. And I had become obsessed with hedgehogs.

I had noticed that my nightly garden-visiting regulars were appearing sluggish. This brought a flash of inspiration to a poser that had been irking me: why in some local churchwarden accounts from 1729 had two shillings and eight pence been paid for forty-seven hedgehogs and a sparrowhawk? Of course, I thought, slugs! There must have been a grave problem that only a small army of fuz-pigs could cure. Now all I had to solve was the question of the sparrowhawk. But perhaps first of all it occurred to me that I needed to get a life.

Almost two decades had passed since making a video documentary, *Exmoor - An English Wild Kingdom*, about which the viewing public had generally been kind. During this time I had abandoned making large squibs with the broadsheet *Guardian*, the altered chemical make-up of its paper had made it fire-resistant. Happily, both the *Independent* and *Observer* remained excellent alternatives. I heaved myself upright from beside the cold-summered iron-lump stove. Having washed my coal-grubby hands, pulled a log splinter from my thumb and whinged about a broken toe stubbed on the banister, I made a decision to emerge from behind my warped blue front door. I would fulfil my promise to Chaggi and make sure all was still well in the world of jodhpurs, antler men and fishers.

However, as three starlings bum-nudged each other on the telephone wire outside the bedroom window, making room for a fourth before chattering a quorum of advice, I was suddenly full of self-doubt. I thought it best to begin things with a visit to my publisher. There was a question I had to ask. I found the chap dapperly dressed like a bright ember in an up-draught, in red tie, red sweater and red socks not forgetting trousers and shoes that shone anthracite black. But he was reluctant ears.

After a nervous cough I ploughed into my concern. It was in the common domain that local police were investigating "damage to a letterbox" belonging to a baddy – a lank-haired brunette lady photographed looking smug sat in a pristine galvanised steel wheelbarrow with a trug and well-washed pooch at her green-wellied feet. Her metal letterbox had been peppered by shotgun pellets in the manner normally reserved for a triangular road sign with a stag silhouette. Indeed, shooting at signs has been a Exmoor pastime ever since 1754 when the sign of the Ship Inn in Porlock became target practice. Back then the pub owner was given 10/6d in compensation.

Lord knows what the brunette wanted as damages. She was a lady author, tabloid columnist and 'furriner' who fed rats and mice on muesli, was allegedly grotty towards locals and who spoke of a "terror attack". Internet blogs were full of the tappings of upset local sensibilities particularly well voiced in *Diary of a Desperate Exmoor Woman* written by a goody who was also a shaman and shortlisted for the Author Blog Awards. These were liberal times.

"Exmoor's been done to death by writers seen as Christ or Anti-Christ," I said. "Do you still really want another let loose on the discerning public?"

"Snell," muttered the Bright Ember.

Possibly taking my sudden frown to be quizzical ignorance, the Bright Ember gave me one of his stares that accompany one of his sighs. "Frederick Snell," he said. "Every book on Exmoor since the year dot, well, 1903, that involves red deer, hunting or history has been a variation on Snell's *Book of Exmoor*. Admittedly with a word changed here or there." Then, looking me up and down taking in my shabby chic of favourite lambskin leather jacket, mud stained chinos, cooking fat stained jumper and tousled hair, added, "Best look at sub-culture and draw from self-experience."

"So, best not let Frederick be my vade mecum." I said, causing the bright ember to raise an eyebrow and me to reconsider.

"Rather than look at the 'toffs' on horses," the Bright Ember continued, "think about those that car cap among the stag hunt followers."

Ah, the Exmoor hub, I mused whimsically, of course. Often left propped against a roadside beech hedge, put there by kind-hearted discoverers, the forlorn car hub cap was as common a sight on Exmoor as road-kills. Many years ago I'd found just such a hub cap beside a poignant slab of newly dried inscribed clay set into a Morebath Hill grassy verge. It read:

> 'POOR OLD RENARD
> BURIED HERE FOILED
> THE HUNTER MANY A
> YEAR A VIXEN CALLED
> ACROSS THIS ROAD
> AND HE FORGOT THE
> GREEN + CODE
> R.I.P.'

I mused of wheel hubs lost in lamented animal collisions or in rocky ruts during the hunt chase being replaced by a supporting capper force. But naturally, the Bright Ember wasn't on about that. Surely he was on about tireless and insistent weathered-hardened hill-farming women. Those that went from battered Land Rover to scratched Subaru to rag-tag followers on quad bikes to collect donations for the staghounds throughout the season, often two or three times a week. They were very good at it. Being acquainted with such ladies was, to my mind, a privilege.

"You mean women like Gwen and Barbara?"

They were the Bawden sisters of Cloggs Farm, who with their nephew David farmed Exmoor horned sheep in traditional fashion and nurtured shaggy hill cattle in straw-warm Hawkridge shippen barns and in fields above the Danes Brook on the Devon and Somerset borderland. Both ladies were in late middle age and the seventh generation of Bawdens at Cloggs. The family had featured in a documentary film I'd made in the mid-1990s. And they were hunters, everyone.

A few generations ago, when tractors were newfangled and had too many tinkerments, a Bawden gained notoriety by whipping a horse out of his plough-team, jumping on its back and following the hunt through half a dozen parishes. And still the family talks of the most famous of Devon and Somerset runs, the 'Glenthorne Day' of 1899 that took place from Hawkridge. A 'two on top' deer, viewed at Three Waters, was chased to the sea cliffs at Glenthorne, a distance of at least sixteen miles. The stag though wasn't 'taken', it jumped. 'Guardsman', a hound, followed after it. Both died on the rocks.

David's father Fred used to tell of Walter, one of the hunt servants, who had his pet theory about scent. Whenever he saw a rainbow in the sky Walter used to stand up in his stirrups and shake his fist with rage, exclaiming: "Darn that thing. There won't be a bit of scent as long as it lasts." And Fred's kinsman, Ernest, is remembered, too. In 1920 Ernest took part in the chase of a hind raised in Allers Wood all the way to Crediton, well, almost. Never before or since have the D&S staghounds run so far southward.

But there was other local history. I remembered Gwen, in red anorak and matching coloured tea cosy hat, had seemed impressed by my snippet of useless knowledge that Danes Brook was anciently called Dunnokesbroke, meaning brook of the hedge-sparrow.

"I suppose it could have been, plenty of them about," she had said before squinting through her spectacles, tutting at the postman's delivery of brown envelopes. Barbara clanged shut a steel gate in exasperation after letting a couple of cows find their calves in the calving byre and have their teats, or as Gwen said, 'lily-hangers', tugged. The cost of living and officious meddlers never made Exmoor living any easier. Such irritations could spoil a day out hunting. And nothing changes apart from the direction of wind gusts that swing the Cloggs weathervane topped by a forge-worked iron stag. Folk just get a little older.

I cast a glance over my cold coffee cup at the Bright Ember to seek assurance that I was on the right track, but his face gave nothing away.

"Car cappers. Absolutely," I said, trying to nod convincingly. It was all part of the social scene, like singing, well, certainly that of the choral variety. And if my information served me well, I knew that in that particular league the Bright Ember was the Simon Cowell of Exmoor. His and many a cajoled and enlisted classical voice could be heard at frequent church entertainment across the moor.

"Are you doing December's Simonsbath church gig?" I asked.

"Maybe. Why?"

"Oh, I could link it to a bit of history about the church being built on the spot where the old Pony Sales used to be held. And subtly drop in the story of the spot also being where Locke of Lynmouth once roasted a buffy bay, mealy nosed Exmoor pony whole for a party of his friends."

"That wouldn't be very wise," said the Bright Ember.

But it was grist for the mill, I thought.

"Oh, by the way, Charles," said the Bright Ember as I made my leaving, "No old wives tales about pirate doubloons being exchanged for haunches of venison."

"Those are just old wives tales?" I queried, feigning incredulity.

"Just remember, I can always scrawl a line through whatever you deliver." No pressure, then.

"How far can I take it?" I said. "I mean how far can Exmoor extend? I've got a great story about a chap keeping a wallaby and some turtles in his bedroom at Tropiquaria. And then there is Jack, an Oxford sandy and black pig who trotted into Williton's housing association offices a couple of months ago. The receptionist thought it was someone coming into to use the computer or pick up some information on swine flu. The piggy was arrested by two policemen. So their next case might have been the shotgun blasted mailbox."

"I leave things to your deliberations," said the Bright Ember with a seemingly heavy heart. "But as a rule of thumb, anything in Snell is generally Exmoor related. And don't go using 'steep', 'hill' or 'inclined' too liberally."

With Porlock Hill and the mineral line at Comberow, this was easier said than done. Some things prove to be just unavoidable.

Behind the relative sanctuary of my warped blue front door I played safe and not wanting expenses to cut too deeply into royalties 'Amazoned' a copy of Frederick for a penny. It arrived from Little Gaddesden Parish church in Hertfordshire - a place incidentally with a pub called the Bridgwater Arms - to chatters, twitters and clicks from the starlings in my eaves, and an honorary guard made up of Peckal, the portly tame hen blackbird, and her cohort of sparrows. On turning the pages I discovered something interesting - old Frederick had included an insight into Exmoor's witchcraft and superstition. Very sub-culture, I thought. Disinterested, my aged whinge-bag of a puss-cat eased herself up onto her cushion to dream of red furrows or mouse flavoured food pouches.

I was good to go.

THREE

Mares' Tails and Picnic Eggs

"The optimist sees the rose and not its thorns; the pessimist stares at the thorns, oblivious to the rose."
    Khalil Gibran, Lebanese essayist, novelist and poet. 1883-1931.

Forty-eight hours later, forewarned and forearmed, I went forth to Selworthy, which but for a debate over a wheelbarrow would probably have been my childhood home. I thought it would be energizing to get some fresh air in my lungs and Selworthy Beacon seemed a wonderful place to inhale it. People had been going there for millennia judging by the series of burial cairns, the grassy iron age ramparts of Bury Castle, or indeed, the sandstone-built Acland memorial hut.

For several years it's tickled me that the beacon has another name – Marilyn. For the trivia minded, Marilyns have peaks and there are one hundred and seventy eight of them in England. To qualify for the name, a peak must be a hundred and fifty metres or more high.

But back to Selworthy. Although the name is an old one that means settlement near willows and had been recorded by quill pen in the Domesday Book as Selewrda, today's village, despite its chocolate boxy appeal of deep thatched roofs, eyebrow dormers and tall chimneys, isn't old at all. Well not in the timeline of history. If truth be told, Selworthy as we know it was created by Sir Thomas Dyke Acland of Killerton in 1828, the same year as the Zoological Gardens at Regent's Park London opened and Casparus van Wooden patented chocolate milk powder.

Sir Thomas was one of a confusion of baronets who could ride from Killerton to Holnicote, a distance of more than thirty miles, without leaving their own land. His son was Sir Thomas and so was his pater, too. So to make things a tad simpler let the Sir Thomas of thatch and tall chimneys be Sir Thomas Ten. A Tory MP for many years, he also gave a nod toward new-fangled progress. In May 1844, Sir Thomas announced to an interested House of Commons that he had left Exeter at 5pm that afternoon and was speaking to the House at 10pm the same day, using the new railway from Exeter. Formerly, it had taken him sixteen to twenty hours by stagecoach. Those who would hanker after a West Somerset Railway could cite potential.

The village design of Selworthy was apparently all Sir Thomas's own work. A romantic philanthropist, he used traditional designs and materials like limewash tinted creamy yellow with ochre to create a deliberately old-fashioned look. All power to him given the modern generation's architectural abominations.

Thomas's aim was to provide housing for the aged and infirm of the Holnicote estate. A little while ago as the hollyhocks bloomed I took tea with a family of journalistic bent in one such cottagy idyll. Surrounded by squished tubes of watercolour, jam jars full of blue-green water, squirrel hair brushes, stained plastic palettes and an easel, Peter Hesp was enjoying retirement while his son Martin carried on the tradition. It was self-evident that Sir Thomas's aim had deviated. Here was now artistic cosiness for incomers. "Hesp means smoked ham in Dutch," Martin laughed.

The trees on the hill above the village and those in the steep valley that shelter the cottage gardens, like Peter's, were planted by Sir Thomas. Perhaps the genial baronet became public spirited after reading Oliver Goldsmith's *Deserted Village* that derived from the 1760s pastoral ballad tradition of drawing on rural description "where health and plenty cheer'd the labouring swain". Yet, in Sir Thomas's world of thatch and trains Orwell's later comment that "progress is not an illusion, but is slow and invariably disappointing" would have possibly left the good chap in a quandary.

Matters were so much easier for his pater, Sir Thomas Nine, Ranger of Exmoor and a man who went by the nickname of 'Prince of the West' who lived for hunting in Exmoor's golden age. He lived at the time when 'Venison Feasts' were held in Porlock to celebrate the end of each stag-hunting season.

During nine seasons as master of the hounds he recorded one hundred and fifty deer, seventy-three of them being stags. And it's said he was killed by grief after his slate-roofed Holnicote manor house was destroyed by fire in 1794 that also melted the family plate. "I care little for the house or the plate," he said, "the one can be rebuilt, the other repurchased. But I am indeed grieved by the loss of my splendid collection of antlers, which I have preserved from stags killed by my own hounds, and which I shall never live to form again." Sir Thomas Nine died a few weeks later and never knew that the Holnicote rebuild would arise from the ashes sporting a roof of thatch.

The nineteenth century writer Richard Jeffries, a man who Henry Williamson regarded as his own alter ego by describing him as "a genius … prophet of an age not yet come into being – the age of sun, of harmony", visited Selworthy shortly before Sir Thomas Eleven's death in 1898. Richard wrote "Selworthy woods were still in the afternoon heat, except for the occasional rustle of a rabbit or of a pheasant, there was no evidence of life; the sound of the sea was faint and soon lost among the ferns. The thatched house at Holnicote by the foot of Selworthy much interested me, it is one of the last of thatched houses inhabited by a gentleman and landed proprietor. Sir Thomas Acland who resides here is a very large owner. Thatch prevails on his estates, thatched cottages, thatched farmhouses, and his thatched mansion. In the cool of the evening the birds begin to sing and squirrels played across the lawn of Holnicote House. Humble bees hummed in the grass and visited the flowers of the holly bushes. Thrushes sang and chaffinches, and, sweetest of all, if simpler in notes, the greenfinches talked and courted in the trees … In the level meadow from among the tall grasses and white flowering wild parsley, a landrail called 'crake, crake' ceaselessly. There is a sense of rest and quiet, and with it joyousness of bird life, such as should be about an English homestead."

To be fair, this paradise was all Sir Thomas Ten's doing. The focal point of his labours had been the fifteenth century church of All Saints distinctive by a modern coat of whitewash. Its tower, I'm led to believe, is a century older. Within the church is a copy of the 1609 chained book by Bishop John Jewel, entitled *Defense of the Apologie of the Church of England* - an attempt to provide a statement of faith for the Church of England under Elizabeth I and answer challenges and accusations of the Romanists against the Protestants. Jewel was a long-nosed, long-faced, thin-bearded chap who had a liking for ruffs and black three-cornered skullcaps and whose black hat and cloak gave him the countenance of a crow. Like the early Protestants, he maintains that Man, because of original sin and his corrupt nature, can produce no good or meritorious works. So where does that leave my newest companion written by Frederick?

Sir Thomas's houses are loosely placed round the long village green that climbs the steep hill towards the God whom man, Jewel believed, must hope and trust in for his salvation. Sunday exercise would obviously do the aged and infirm good, Sir Thomas might have thought. But was there any mischievous intent in him, like for instance, causing death by exhaustion, so keeping Selworthy's housing list ticking over? There has to be some reason to explain why his statue, resplendent in stone greatcoat, now beside the city wall in Northernhay Gardens in Exeter, has had such an unlucky time suffering severe damage by gale and beheading by vandalism, not to mention being a convenience for pigeons. We all collect karma, some say.

Today, with the village population nearly eighty per cent 'saga age' Goldsmith's words still have relevance as the National Trust shop in Perriwinkle Cottage sells life's costly inessentials:

"But now the sounds of population fail,
No chearful murmurs fluctuate in the gale,
No busy steps the grass-grown foot-way tread,
For all the bloomy flush of life is fled."

In life, we, like the media, cotton on to anniversaries. Forty years ago Exmoor first leapt into my own ten-year-oldish whippersnapper psyche when Joy and Maurice, my Mum and Dad, became smitten with the moors' purple heather as my sister, eight years older than me, was doing her own thing. Back in the late Summer of 1972, after sitting on a Acland memorial hut bench and having picnicked on boiled eggs and pork pie, I remember watching Exmoor ponies disturbing ticks in the bracken as the words of America's *Horse with No Name* went round and round inside my head. Mum said the views were lovely, while Dad observed mares' tails portending rain and storm. His gaze was drawn not to the ponies but to those wispy clouds that are shaped like equine rear appendages.

It's fair to say that Dad was a weather pessimist, an all-weather-grumbler and an avid listener to the BBC's forebodings on television and radio from where he absorbed his highs and lows. For some reason, the long-wave shipping forecast, albeit from a time before Finistere became Fitzroy and Exmoor shippen barns were tidied of their cattle and owls to become double-glazed, rayburn warmed 'des res' for monied city types, always made his world a little better. What would really make him rub his hands together and reach for the sherry bottle were broadcasts like: "Southeast Iceland North 7 to severe gale 9. Heavy snow showers. Good, becoming poor in showers. Moderate icing."

Lundy though was different - the exception to the rule of inclement grottiness. The word 'Lundy' caught Dad's imagination. He used to trip it around his tongue and whisper it under his breath. Any mention of the Bristol Channel rock-pile refuge of pirates, puffins and guillemots that was a blanket hugging, pale-faced, puke-inducing, wave-riding-propeller-visible boat journey away, from Exmoor's rugged coast made him hopeful of life without his thermals. This had ever been the case since Dad caught Frank Muir and Denis Norden parodying the Shipping Forecast in a song written for BBC radio's *Take It From Here*, broadcast well before my time:

"In Ross and Finistère
The outlook is sinisterre
Rockall and Lundy
Will clear up by Monday."

Oh yes, Exmoor offered mild climes despite suffering a lot of wind with the trees tending to lean away from it, much like guests at a dinner party from an unfortunate suffering the consequences of a casserole concocted from well-hung game. And it was a tree that clinched matters for Dad. He spotted a palm in Porlock. Something to do with the Labrador current. I later learned that there were a lot of labradors on Exmoor, and that both they and the clouds piddled a lot.

So, Exmoor beckoned us. Dad believed he could cope with it. That rare sunny holiday had fuelled his soft-centred notions of rural Utopia. Exmoor became the place to where he suddenly wanted to escape. And he needed a change of lifestyle.

A small man, Dad, MBE, Yorkshireman and neatly moustachioed army officer, was rank-stuck. Fed up by being repeatedly passed over to fill bigger boots and having to put up with his polished size seven shoes, he had decided on early retirement from Her Majesty's Royal Engineers. He craved workbench amateurism, honing woodwork skills with chisels and saws to making tenon-joints and dovetails for suitable 'projects'. Mum had simply harboured dreams of the sea, a shady garden tree and walking to a village shop for food rather than to the NAAFI. Well, Exmoor would have fulfilled two out of three. On Exmoor I feared we would starve.

However, for me it came as a shock that as a family we were heading for 'The Darkness'. Even now from Georgeham to Roadwater one can only hope for clear skies and moonlight to make one's way around many a village lane and byway. Torches are life essentials. I mean, heavens, Stoke Pero homes didn't enjoy electricity from the National Grid until the late 1990s.

Not even Looking Glass's *Brandy* courtesy of Radio Luxembourg could soothe my anxiety when my parents decided on buying half of the old Selworthy rectory. Different to the other village houses, it was in keeping with the church by having a slate roof, although the church's seemed in better repair. Available to buy for less than it cost to buy my bargain of a dented second-hand Skoda today, the half rectory unfortunately wasn't the better half. Yes, both bits had mossy green gardens for and aft, but on the other side of the green dividing tangle-hedge was a driveway front to back that would have given access to a horse and cart, well at least a Vauxhall Viva. On what was to potentially be our side it was impossible to even get a wheelbarrow around.

I remember overhearing the conversation as Dad and Mum lay on their bed in Minehead's Plume of Feathers hotel before it was demolished for flats. Dad puffed on his pipe filled with Exmoor Gold deep in contemplation. Mum fiddled with a knitting needle. The *Daily Telegraph's* back page quick cross-word lay unattended.

"We'll have to take the blasted thing through the kitchen and down the hallway," declared Dad.

"Why couldn't we buy two wheelbarrows?" asked Mum, helpfully.

"Don't be silly, Joy. We'll have to find somewhere else."

"Oh, Maurice."

When I returned to Selworthy behind my car steering wheel, I noticed that two thatchers were keeping up standards. I knew them. They were notorious for their cocks. Not that they were anything lewd, merely outsized thatch birds tied onto roofs with spars and wires. Paul and Matthew enjoyed 'experimenting' and were of that new breed dressed more urban than rustic. With their designer wear and immaculately shaved stubble only their worn knee-pads gave a hint to them being traditional artisans, apart, of course, from the abundant sheaves of trimmed reeds. I had gleaned from Matthew that the reeds were of a special kind of wheat that grows about a metre tall. "One of the prettiest sights on Exmoor has to be a field of ripe wheat that's been cut and stood in stooks," he had said. I have to agree with him.

After a wave and a thumbs up to the lads, I pootled passed the old rectory that has also been done up and parked by the church. Deciding to consult Frederick on his Selworthy thoughts I noted that he called Sir Thomas Nine 'the Eighth', which only added to the confusion of baronets. But I took the Bright Ember's point about word changing here or there. What else did Frederick have to say? What better than a ghost story that he had 'borrowed' from a Mr Thornton's *Reminiscences of an Old West Country Clergyman*.

The story concerned a "stout, ruddy and free from fancy" thirty-five year old called Mary Stenner, who lived in the farmhouse by the church. She had seen a "nasty thing" running along beside her when she was out walking. From her account, it had "four legs, was black and had great fiery eyes as big as saucers, and," she claimed, "it ran on until it came to where the water crosses under the road, and they things, of course, never can abide running water, so it couldn't get across, and off it went up in the air like a flash of fire."

Further enquiries were made and it seems the church sexton knew all about the awful spectre. Twenty-five years earlier he had been involved in bringing the corpse of somebody or other from Horner Mill to Selworthy, when the handle of the coffin 'against the head' came loose at the very spot Mary met her apparition. The sexton had picked up a stone and knocked the handle in again, and he was in little doubt it went into the brain and let the spirit out.

Blimey, what if some local wag had told me the story all those years ago, worrying my impressionable head? Certainly, on closing Frederick's book for the time being, I was ever so pleased the hypothetical wheelbarrow had saved me from potential heebie-jeebies in the 'Darkness'.

Gazing down in the valley I saw that Luccombe was in great Dunkery's evening shadow. Getting out of the car I decided on a short wander. A small shaggy dog greeted me, adding extra mud to my chinos before a hearty lady in a blue anorak could trill "Oh, Moppy, come here!"

In the churchyard a large fat cock pheasant with white parson collar strutted between the gravestones and rabbit droppings, wood-pigeons cooed and rooks cawed in their deliberate way. Nostalgic? Well, undoubtedly for the world of Richard Jeffries. With doffs of hats and tugs of forelocks, the spirits of Holnicote estate workers, as well as the odd coffin creature, would still recognise Sir Thomas Ten's creation that's preserved among his trees.

With the day turning dimpsey there was no time to ascended my Marilyn. Instead I headed home to Wivey's streetlights and a washing machine. I was relieved that Exmoor didn't seem to have drastically changed. So had I worried for nothing? It was early days.

Barrow Pigs and Street Beasts

"Years wrinkle the skin, but to give up enthusiasm wrinkles the soul."
Douglas MacArthur, American General, 1880-1964.

With October's leaves spinning and tumbling towards Halloween, bullfinches and tits devouring the fat balls in green nylon nets decorating the patio hawthorn skedaddled. A rap on my warped blue front door signalled that James, a sporting young GP finding himself between relationships, had turned up with a chainsaw and a brace of bunnies. The shade inducing beech tree that overhung my garden wall required his surgical skills and he knew my wife and I had a liking for rabbit casserole.

James in turn wanted to vent life's frustrations by way of arboreal massacre and by creating a bonfire inferno that would obliterate patchy grass and lawn moss. Then, as I was being smoked out of house and home together with a pair of collared doves and a squirrel, I remembered it was the last Thursday in the month. I should be somewhere else. I should be in Bampton. This was the date that the pubs had their windows removed in case of guddler brawls and Exmoor ponies came unwillingly to town. Gawd help me, it was Fair Day, a calendar event since the early thirteenth century.

Coughing James a farewell and spluttering something akin to "don't earn me an ASBO", I took the car, turned left by the traffic lights, and followed the bonnet into rain. Beyond Somerset's border patrols of weasels, where the road became uneven with neglect, lay a skeleton cupboard of Deb'n memories. By heading for Bampton I was continuing my chase of ghosts – those formative years of enthusiastic youth when you appreciate that having a wheelbarrow is truly an essential part of existence.

It's peculiar how you can wake up one morning and realise, blimey, I've spent a quarter of a century of my life muddling through in one place, almost becoming part of the fabric of evolution. Well, that was me and Bampton. Yes, I did eventually escape to a less hassled existence, but not before my children had discovered the woes of being prodded from beneath warm duvets on dark frosty mornings to egg collect or to feed and muck out an accumulated menagerie of feathered, furred and hoofed livestock, most of it unplanned.

I still recall small voices made loud by indignation: "No, I won't. It's Lawrence's job to catch the peacocks." "It's Maddy's turn to fetch the sneezy straw." "Daddy, Ez won't pick up Moppet's egg 'cos it's covered in poo." "Dad, Felix won't let the geese out anymore. Gerald chased him." "Dad, the sheep's in your bedroom. Dad!" My head spins as I recollect, ever so glad that our fauna is now reduced to a goldfish and a street-tart cat.

The problem with having space is that other people know that you have it and take advantage. A matter made worse by an inability to say no. For instance, those peafowl, Desmond and Desdemona, came as a gift from a affable Morebath chap whose smirk I mistook for a smile. Who was I to know such pretty birds would eat the chemist's petunias, make a God-awful racket cross-between an industrial buzzer and the bray of a donkey from the top of our chimney stacks, or be fired at by a lunatic with a shotgun from the housing estate up on the hill?

Gerald, a Brecon buff goose, and his two 'ladies' arrived as a present from John, my youngest son's guddling godfather, who, when regrettably defrocked as a vicar, was asked to vacate his rectory. The birds turned out to be vicious leg-biting predators.

Two lop-eared rabbits became escapees joining the hillside burrow of grey commoners, with interesting results. On the other hand, the feather-puff Pekins, the Old Dutch and the Furness bantams, that produced eggs with the rapidity of Gatling guns, were nervous stay-at-homes being on the menu of rats. Juxtaposed, knackered ex-battery brown warren hens with floppy red combs, brought with 50p pocket money, somehow found the energy to lay breakfast, before expiring with the effort.

Jeremy, the geriatric Buff Orpington duck, however, had more lives than a cat. I once sighted him a distance away playing 'dead-duck' in a fox's jaws. The duck gained salvation only after I hit the captor up the backside with a hastily whanged trowel. As the fox opened its mouth to protest Jeremy made his frantic flap-flap-flap to freedom.

Things got dafter with the arrival of a pair of malevolent goats who believed if something didn't move it was edible. Consequently they put Lawrence, my eldest, in A. & E., needing stitches in his unmentionables. Thereafter, milking time became a mission beyond the call of duty for any of my children.

And, of course, there was Mary, Farmer Rawle's runt lamb, which grew up to be bouncy and big. It was only a thought, but maybe Mary had Bampton in her blood. Frederick, I noticed, mentioned that the Bampton was once a pure breed of sheep described as "the best in Devon," something which might have imbued Mary with her survivability. The Royal Agricultural Society's Journal of 1855 offset this theory, however, by stating "the meat is juicy". Regularly reminding Mary of this fact kept her face the whitest white.

By keeping Mary and the rest of the adopted creatures in mind, my relief is profound that during that duvet prodding time the fair's pony sales had thankfully demised. Had they not, it wouldn't have been a case of 50p here or there, piggy banks would have ceased to rattle in hope of a set of dainty hoofs more lasting than "cups of steel".

What got imposed on us instead was Poppy, a brown mongrel of a pony who came with her friend, an equally mongrelly chicken. Both were homeless due, apparently, to some dispute over rent. I disputed Poppy's right to trit-trot undaintily through the flowerbeds and make a paddock for herself on the front lawn. My mum would have turned in her grave.

Personally, I abrogated all responsibility. None of this was my fault. Dad had just been in the wrong place at the wrong time and saw the 'For Sale' notice for a Bampton property. I meekly went with the flow. It was only years later that I was fated to be left impecuniously in charge of his white elephant. And whilst retaining many a mixed feeling about the town, I came to understand early on that Bampton was a place that provoked subjective opinions.

Neither bell-bottom jeans and Doc Martins, nor yeti coat and kaftan had been for me. As a teenager I needed to address my image. I wanted to keep my allowance by meeting with Dad's approval. He desired that I be passed off as a young rural gentleman.

Pocketing my first chequebook I went to Dulverton. Having handed a scribbled promissory note over to the attentive bearded chap in Hills outfitters, I was given a plastic bag containing a tweed sports jacket and tweed flat cap in return. Next was the haircut. It's strange how one gives away little details when sat in a salon chair. "Oh, you live in Ponyville," said the sleeveless-puffer-jacketed woman with the scissors. "You know, Bampton always reminds me of a northern mining town."

Not having been particularly well travelled myself at the time, I couldn't really contradict her. However, I knew where she was coming from. As a place it had a certain edge. From the top of Bampton's motte and bailey where King Stephen hung an archer for reasons best known to himself, one could see Exmoor. And at the castle's foot one could watch the ponies playing football. Seriously. The 'Ponies' was the nickname of the town's football team. Many a time Reg Gutteridge, the postmaster, tried his level best with wayward deliveries into the oppositions box. But these were the few high points.

Below the football pitch, Bampton sits in a steep sided hollow. From late autumn through winter and into early spring, coal smoke and wood smoke drifted from chimneys and hung over the town's grey stone shops and dwellings like a pall that was added to by quarry dust. In Victorian times the local quarries provided most of the employment and Bampton was a noisy, dusty industrial place.

Indeed, while bemoaning the disappearance of "the ruined forge, with its moss covered roof" and many a thatched cottage, Frederick himself noted that Bampton "has been much modernised, and is no longer the quaint old place that it once was." Blame, he opined, indeed lay with the "Cyclopean quarries".

During the 1970s every weekday town windows shook as explosions like rumbling thunderclaps rent the air, as a hillside was blasted. The quarries worked overtime producing 120,000 tons of stone for Clatworthy's reservoir dam and 200,000 tons for Wimbleball's.

And of course, at home, there were the pits. Once filled with lime and nasties in various degrees of dilution, they were called 'suspenders' and 'floaters' and were for dunking raw animal skins, not for hacking at coal in.

Let me add a little more light. Early retirement took longer than Dad imagined after the Selworthy wheelbarrow conundrum, however, a project for his artisan fervour was found and Mum was enchanted by a view of a pretty orchard of apple trees that dripped mistletoe on the overlooking hill.

A request was made to my Granny Mary. She had been an independent young woman who had ridden across North America on mule back, something remarkable for an Englishwoman so many years ago. From a decayed and frayed family of aristos repressed into silence and where humour rarely smiled, Granny perceived emotion as a weakness that had to be suppressed. Hers was a fading England. The battlefields of oblivion had claimed first her two officer brothers and then her pilot son, my Mum's brother. But the positive was that she still had available funds.

Due to her contribution and stiff upper lip the old defunct Frog Street Tannery became a bargain home for Dad, Mum, my sister, myself and a golden retriever named Honey. Granny got offered an upstairs room or two in which to spend her last days.

However, within weeks of us all moving in, the view of the orchard vanished. It was grubbed up and gone. Cement mixers churned and concrete foundations were laid for what was to become the gun toting housing estate. Dad chuntered about the vendors withholding local knowledge and Mum considered net curtains.

Like Holnicote tannery and others in the Exmoor area, in its Victorian pomp our place wouldn't have been for the faint hearted. Flies, putrid pongs, arsenic and stream poisoning came with the charm of de-fleshing and de-hairing, stretching, drying and currying. The latter being nothing to do with cow hide korma, but was instead a rather violent pummelling of butt and belly skins with oil and tallow in the tan yard that gave them 'pliability' and, hopefully, quality.

The skins had come by the horse-drawn cartload from abattoirs. Sessile oaks in the Batherm and Exe valleys were coppiced and their bark high in tannin was stripped, dried and brought for storing in the bark house over the bridge crossing the stream of Shuttern Brook at the bottom of the garden, back then a rancorous flow. Amazingly, this was at the time when there were aspirations of elevating Bampton to spa status based on a claim that the waters of a town well were of the same quality as Harrogate, despite them resembling liquid rust. The fanciful notion had prompted the local medical health officer,

Dr Thomas Guinness, the great-great-grandson of the founder of Dublin's Guinness brewery, to have the idea of selling the water in bottles. Iron, he assured, was fortifying. Unsurprisingly, locals didn't touch a bottle with a barge pole, nor for that matter did anyone else. And a Spar became preferred to a spa.

By the time I took my first stream paddle, the once toxic had evolved into water of paradisiacal innocence. Mallards and their ducklings bank-snoozed or bobbed in the shallow eddies. Small, shrimp-like beasties lived under stones, troutlings swam and kingfishers flashed. Gate-crashing this tranquillity, mink were vicious marauders.

As for the lime pits, several had been covered over by embankment soil when the railway came in 1884 linking Dulverton to Tiverton and the world beyond until the day Beeching scuppered things in 1963. Nothing grew on that spot of pits save for grass. Any planted tree died, its thrusting roots poisoned. The whole smelly process was not something Mum ever discussed at dinner parties. Never did she mention her difficult suspenders. No, her line was, "Oh, did you know, during the war our house was a boarding school?"

She didn't lie. The dormitories were in the barn where the reeking skins had once dried. That must have been nice. We got them full of rats, bats and mice. My sister bought herself an extra furry yeti coat and left home for good. A barmaid's job in a distant remote village offered her better hope for the future.

Yet Dad had his project, an investment worth gentrifying. Mum had a challenge. To be honest, as a property it was a little the worse for wear. A Devon longhouse of sorts, it was replete with several water features, both natural and unnatural. At a distance the house looked green, close up it was painted white but covered in moss and algae, a damp pile of stone and friable cob full of wheeze-making straw. A leat ran through the foundations, frogs hopped in hallway and sitting room. Slugs and their slime trails were ever-present carpet decorations. Mouse droppings were laid nightly behind the plates and jam jars in the larder. Doorframes and windowsills were daddicky to the finger prod. And if you were very quiet for a minute, you could hear the a-gnawing 'tic-tic-tic' sound of xestobium rufovillosum, better known as death watch beetle.

As the novelties wore off, the odd jobs Dad began not involving woodchip wallpaper and tins of magnolia he never finished. A door may have got a knob, but seldom a catch. He retreated beaten to the extensive gardens to commence new battles.

Tall stone walls hid a front garden inherited with blighted spuds, bolted carrots, dandelions, daisies and forget-me-nots with a centrepiece of the most beautiful age-twisted Bramley apple tree you ever did see. It was a tree that became the hub of sanity and sweet cider swigging as slowly, backachingly, fork thrust by fork thrust, spud carrot and 'weed' gave way to rose beds and a seeded lawn that softly, sneakily, turned to moss.
.
In failing health, and while Dad grew her sweet peas and regimented rows of vegetables that would end up lying bagged and uneaten in the chest freezer, Mum named the apple tree her 'Koolaba' and relished its shade in summer heat as she lounged upon her one time fashion statement – a 1960s' red and white plastic and aluminium recliner.

Despite her never having seen any specimen of the white barked growth of the Australian outback or known the words to *Walzing Matilda*, "sitting under the koolaba tree" was a phrase she'd picked up from the age of manners and etiquette. Whilst a billy can would no doubt have seemed something quite romantic to Mum, her preference was for the Crown Derby china tea-service wintered and autumned in a glass panel cabinet. Such refinement, however, occasionally got mislaid when, as a lady who couldn't whistle, Mum made a noise like a demented owl, 'ooohoo-ooohoo', when calling the dog that showered earth and clumps of cherished grass in its frenetic digs for garden moles.

Beyond Mum's 'Koolaba', in a gloomy walled corner, a ginormous yew enveloped a streetlight struggling to assist pickled night meanderers.

One such was Derek. Wiry, thin moustached and with a penchant for wearing a shabby deerstalker hat, he lived with his wife in the row of tin-pot houses up the street. Built during World War II, these pre-fabs with their metal frames and curved corrugated iron roofs were intended to last no more than ten years, but folk just got used to them and put the long garden plots they came with down to veg and chicken coops. Derek was no exception and kept a rooster with the loudest crow in Christendom and which cock-a-doodle-dooed at the oddest hours.

Eventually Derek was the last employee to be laid off by old Mrs Scott, the endmost quarry owner, as the industry dwindled away.

It was Derek who told me about 'spring button', an innocuous low-alcohol Exmoor beer that, he believed, could be drunk until all a fellow's buttons flew off, before it affected the head. I have to confess to never having tried it.

Neither, I believe, did Derek. To his detriment, he was a guddler with a weakness for the local cider. Bampton cider was infamous in the area and sold exclusively at the White Horse, a pub that had been a firm favourite of the Mayor of London Boris Johnson's grandparents while on their annual visit to see his father, Stanley, boarding at Ravenswood School.

At least once a month Derek could be found between the pub and the tin-pots, lying prostrate under our streetlamp, his feet pointing in the direction of home. Before Dad and I would take an arm each he would look hazily upwards, attempt a salute and slur "Private 379582. Sir!"

At the click of his front gate a bedroom window would fly open and his wife would shout: "'Derek! What'ya bin doin'!"

"Oh woman, stop yer clitter-to-clatter!" he would holler back. All as regular as groundhog day.

When sober, Derek would act as if nothing amiss had ever happened. Instead, he regaled gelignite tales of the explosive being carried from its safe keeping in middle of Bampton to the quarries, strapped to the cross-bar of a bicycle. And if rendered unstable by sub-zero temperatures, being warmed by blokes round their stove. He evoked stories of gangrenous limbs, abrupt leavings from the mortal coil, as well as the joys of spring.

But I knew there had been quarry victims. 'Two Fingers' Fred was one. His allotment that separated our drive of weeds from the tin-pots was in my Dad's words "a junk yard". Fred, though, always seemed happiest pottering in it, yearly producing mega-marrows awarded with red rosettes at the summer fête. How he won the plaudits remained his secret, which only went to annoy Dad even more.

It was Derek who imparted the informative. When the coal and oil lorries had an impasse in the narrow street causing much arm flapping and heated argument, Derek might give me a nudge and comment, "Know them useful passin' places yous gets in country lanes that yous 'aven't got 'ere? That's where Bampton quarry stone was tipped. Piles of the stuff it were, fer the bleddy stonebreaker. The gurt machine 'ammered the stone to lumps the size of m'fist an' spread un all across the way. Then the roller come along an' squashed the stone into the mud. It made a road, yer see." It was a most enlightening snippet of knowledge. I often bring it to mind whenever I whack into reverse, playing second fiddle to oncoming tractors, horseboxes, milk tankers, delivery vans and motorists of certain natures.

Derek was joined in the ranks of guddlers by Gordon. His weakness was registered in his bulbous red nose and no doubt in his liver. Always wheezing as though on death's door, he, too, had worked the quarries, but had turned his large hands to other activities. A genial rogue of infinite patience and skill, Gordon, of gypsy blood and a self-confessed poacher, was as adept at wringing the neck of a pheasant or rabbit as he was at laying a hedge in the old Devon way of 'tying in' or rebuilding a crumbled stone wall. And at hedging and walling he was a marvel. Agreeing to hourly rates he considered "most reasonable", Gordon busied himself on Dad's 'project'. Hazels were tamed and crumbling garden walls made sound. However, his time with us coincided with the reported disappearance of Derek's irritating rooster. "Must be mink," said Gordon with a wink.

As Gordon helped Dad, so Queenie, also with Gypsy genes, helped Mum with household chores, attired in a nylon blue housecoat. Many gypsies, Gordon included, Queenie explained, came to Bampton because of the fair and ended up staying, giving up a nomadic lifestyle for bricks and mortar permanence. Indeed, she had drawn her first breath a hundred yards down our street in one of the tiny Frog Street cottages that these days have names like *Tadpole* or the slightly macabre *Croak*.

Diminutive and as wrinkled as a dry prune, Queenie, a grandmother whose daughter had moved "longaways to Bristol", had a heart of gold, as well as the gift of gossip. "Oh, did you hear Reverend Clarridge ate a daffodil during the Easter sermon?" she once confided, adding that she had delighted in what followed being more a case of regurgitation than resurrection. The oddball story was par for a church whose tower bore an epitaph to a child who died accidentally: "Bless my iiiiiis, Here he lies, In a sad pickle, Killed by icicle, In the year 1776."

"Bet t'wasn't little 'un's parents who came up wi' that," Queenie had giggled. One had to take note, as it seemed everything Queenie uttered turned out to be true. Bless her, she had the gift of 'seeing' and believed in alectromancy, claiming she could divine a chap's fortune from patterns a cockerel randomly revealed by pecking at a pile of corn. Resorting to a tin of *Green Giant*, I tipped its contents onto the floor tiles and foolishly let her have a go with Chaunte-cleer, my weather-soft pet Furness bantam, who liked to live in the kitchen, the warmest place on his Earth.

Queenie studied intently as the bird obliged her, stuffing itself greedily. Before too long she informed me, rather alarmingly at my tender age, that I was cursed. "But dunna worry," she added, "curses wear off." But obviously I worried. Yet, by now I think, any such curse must surely be wearing thin, unless of course it was related to penury. Hope remains to this day, however, that Chauntecleer was dyslexic.

Be that as it may, coming with our dilapidated outbuildings, unloved stables and parcel of land, we also got Ernie Neeve, a peppercorn tenant. He came with the property purchase deal, a reason for the 'bargain'. With us he kept his workshop, vegetable patch and pig. He was 'come-by-chance', he asserted, the result of too many grouse in the Staghunters, and born under a Brendon hedge.

I have to confess that twenty years later I, too, had an encounter with a Brendon hedge. And again it was the fault of the Staghunters. I was sober amidst a packed bar of bibblers when a small, slightly sozzled and toothless Exmoor character called Jim Sanders staggered upright to sing *The Exmoor Hunting Song*. Bless his cotton socks, he made the desire to bibble irresistible. Sadly, I didn't just bibble, I guddled.

The news was later brutally broken to me by a disconcertingly unconcerned friend that while lying on my back upon a hedge mattress of damp leaves, my hands holding a woozy head, I became a discordant embarrassment singing:

> "Hark to the tufters' challenge true,
> 'Tis a note that the red-deer knows!
> His courage awakes; his covert he breaks,
> And up for the moor he goes!
> He's all his rights and seven on top,
> His eye's the eye o a king,
> And he'll beggar the pride of some that ride
> Before he leaves the ling!
> So hurry along, the stag's afoot,
> The Master's up and away!
> Halloo! Halloo! we'll follow it through
> From Bratton to Porlock BaAAAY!"

Like old Jim, Ernie was always stubble-bearded and had a face lined with the wisdom of age; and he knew what was what. The cobwebbed mill stone leaning against a barn wall, for instance, was once used for making tannin liquor by grinding oak bark and not, as Dad had thought, for squishing cider apples.

Ernie's cobble-floored workshop was, he chuckled, his place of escape from his red-cheeked smiley-faced missus who kept him "snug as a toad under a pair of chain harrows." That's to say, under the thumb. Oh, the poor old long-suffering lad.

Should any Bamptonian's tool handle became detached from its purpose, Ernie would make a repair using a pedal lathe, adze, chisel and mallet, so that it would be, as he described it, "tight as a bullock's prick up a vicar's arse". Nothing was too far gone. Nothing was thrown away. Ernie was a fixer. Floor strewn fork ends and rake tines entangled themselves with spades and rusted shears. Boxes of flat-ended nails, screws, nuts and bolts, and pointy iron bits of unknown usage were plonked in squinches and upon rickety shelves, all nicely at hand for a rummage. I liked Ernie.

His bucket-and-chuck-it flushed to a septic tank at the bottom of the garden above which grew a profuse carpet of snowdrops, always in flower by the last week of January. They were followed in mid-summer by bushes that dripped with the plumpest goozegogs.

Never asking Ernie about his diet, I first got chatting to him when he was at the Savoy – not London's most iconic luxury hotel, but a flourishing cabbage in his own vegetable patch. He was attacking it with a sheath knife, cutting off the larger outer leaves to first iron them and then tie them onto his knees normally hidden by worse-for-wear trousers held up by braces. The leaves helped his arthritis when the sage and crushed mothballs failed. For him cabbage was one of nature's wonders, much like a stick of rhubarb being grand for cleaning a horse brass.

After his missus, Ernie's greatest love was Harold, a reasonably sized pink pig with high testosterone penned up in a roughshod concrete block sty in the old bark house. The only other Harold I've ever known was my Grandad. Sadly, the only memory I have of him was his nicking the cherry off my sister's trifle and making her cry. The pig was much more endearing, especially when Ernie got regular invitations from a neighbourly farmer beyond the tin-pots for Harold to cover one of his sows. What followed was a well-practiced art.

Collecting his wobbly-wheeled, rust-holed, wheelbarrow on route, Ernie would saunter down to Harold. As the pig heard the bump, bump of the barrow wheel coming over the stream bridge, Harold would go slightly mental with oinks and throaty snuffle-grunts as he head-banged his sty door. Unlatched, a gleeful Harold would plonk himself at one end of the wheelbarrow as Ernie tilted it downwards and then ease himself backwards as his master righted it, like a counterweight. Then they were off, happy pig and bandy-legged man. "Cor, 'arold don't 'alf loike gettin' 'is oats," said Ernie to me one day, in passing. The sight was a lesson that wheelbarrows weren't just about practicalities; sitting in one meant sex.

Yes, Harold was part of Ernie's routines in the same way as he daily lit a blaze in a stone built fireplace upon which a large copper of water provided copious cups of tea and washing facilities. However, on Bampton Fair day the fire under Ernie's copper went cold as the town turned beastly.

For me the eve of the fair caused tingles of excitement for a break from the ordinary. Bampton battened down the hatches as the 'fair folk' arrived with their accents of Cockney, Midlands and the North. The landlord of the White Horse supervised window removal and worried over his barrels of ale and cider. The shouts from street vendors mixed with the clang of the steel frameworks of stalls. A melee of tarpaulins and trestles were struggled with. Boxes of stock, be they 'Country and Western' cassettes, sheepskins, cheap plastic toys, crocus bulbs or wooden handcrafted dibbers, would be kept locked up in vans or slept beside. Fair lorries with grinding gears and painted signage declaring "as seen on TV" manoeuvred into position. They would sell factory seconds teapots or dodgy electricals offered by blokes bawling "an absolute steal and I'll give it to you for not ten, not eight, but for just five pounds" into microphones. Then the pubs began to crowd, the first punch was thrown and the air filled with anticipation for the morrow. Perhaps it would even be dry. Fat chance.

With the sore heads, drizzle and downpours came the ponies. And Ernie was on hand to help out and soothe. Let me quote Frederick Snell as to why:

"In the sale-ring the little frightened pony is like a cork in a bucket of water. Round and round he goes, and to and fro, utterly mystified as to what is expected of him, and wholly a creature of impulse. After a while the hammer falls, and then a space is cleared for the pony's escape. Out he flies amidst a rain of blows, and is immediately lodged in the 'sold' ring ...The Exmoor pony, though some have praised his docility, does not entirely merit the compliment – least of all in his wild, untutored state. In Mr Blackford's yard a 'sucker,' held by two men, was awaiting its turn to be sold, when, without the slightest warning, it fixed its hind-legs against a hurdle, rose on end, and turned a somersault. Its keepers, dragged after it, were pitched into an adjoining plot."

For my part, wary of the show of white in the eyes I made my excuse to Ernie of "being allergic" and kept my distance from the plunging, rearing, squealing, kicking mass of the absolutely terrified.

The first ponies that showed their noses in Bampton in 1856 were those that remained unsold at the Brendon Pony Fair that took place on the third Saturday in October. Given Ernie's birthplace, I quipped whether he drifted to Bampton with the ponies. He never denied it.

The ponies were originally sold at pitches throughout the streets and shared space with cattle and sheep. But because of the seething crowds and street beasts doing what comes naturally, like 'port-of-calls' and causing carnage, the pony sales eventually became restricted to an orchard behind a pub and the cattle and sheep got the boot.

The travel writer Laurence Meynell admits to buying a pony that he had no great desire for, nor any immediate means of dealing with. In his defence he claimed that he did the deed due to the over-persuasive tongue of "a Romany" and whilst under the mellowing effects of Bampton ale. He wrote that the pony "was one of the true Exmoor sort; mealy-nosed, as tough as whipcord, as wild as a hawk and more obstinate than the Devil himself". Luckily he sold the beast, at a slight profit, before the end of the day.

Along with the bids for ponies bookings were taken by the Moor Bailiff for Exmoor summer grazing between 1st May and 7th October the following year, proof that the fair really was an important farming community affair.

Now the pony sales have returned. In 2003 a mare and foal whinnied about town, courtesy of the Exmoor Pony Society and a year later a small pony sale returned when over twenty-four horses and ponies were sold at auction for prices ranging from around £80 to £2,400.00 at the new local venue of Luttrell Farm.

By the time I pitched up on the afternoon of James's conflagration and wedged my car into an inconvenient space the pony sales were well and truly over. And folk clinging onto balloons, candyfloss and 'bargains' of tut were puddle-splashing their way home. Those that didn't headed for the helter-skelters, dodgems and the more vomit-inducing rides, much as they did back when I bought my tweed.

After finding my own bargain of crocus bulbs, I took a nostalgic stroll up Frog Street. The old tannery looked very smart in a coat of pristine white-wash. New double-glazed windows, gloss black painted wrought iron rail-ings and an expensive conservatory revealed a couple of barn conversions. Not an animal stirred. No sight of a wheelbarrow or a driveway weed. My Dad never had the vision to realise such a dream, he like me, endured the 'character'.

As I reached the car, the first owl of evening hooted 'oohoo-oohoo' and I was overcome by an overwhelming sense of sadness. When we have been blessed to experience the love and protection of strong and profound family ties in our life, we become aware of how precious and unique this love is in these 'modern' times, when families and friendships are falling apart. We look around and realize that it would not be possible to replace these deep love and bonds once our loved ones are gone from our lives – when they die, when they move away, when for some reason or another they go out of our exis-tence. And with this awareness we develop deep fears of separation. Bampton was indeed a place of ghosts.

A few days later I returned to Bampton, summoned by a doctor's reception-ist, saying I was "due for a jab". Whilst I sat gazing absentmindedly at the nicely framed watercolour memories of quarry slag heaps and rusted iron shacks that hung on the surgery's waiting room wall a husky smoker's voice beside me said, "Charles? Bloody hell, I thought you were dead!"

"Roy"' I responded with astonishment. "I thought you were dead, too."

"What a pair of survivors, eh? What a pair of survivors."

FIVE

Fangs, Whizzes and Geminids

"By night, an atheist half believes in God."
Edward Young, English poet 1681-1765.

At first glance, through the tired eyes of evening, I thought the piece in the week's *Somerset County Gazette* concerned a new sighting of the Exmoor Beast. Blimey, it had only been ten months since the last one.

But that had been more of a tripping over than a sighting. A woman had reported finding a rotting black furred creature "the size of a calf with canine teeth" washed up near Croyde Bay and had used the B-word. The carcass turned out to be a metre and half long with a once powerful chest. The teeth grabbed folks' attention. Great fangs jutted from a huge jaw. So one thing was probably on the minds of Sergeant Jeff Pearce and PC Chris Tucker when they were called to investigate the fearsome but long-dead whatever-it-was. Had the Exmoor Beast met its end? Certainly, the corpse was too big for a dog or domestic cat and too small for an Exmoor pony. It couldn't have been a cow, the teeth were all wrong. What about a seal? Nope, the thing had legs. Surely it was the elusive puma. Or was it a jaguar?

A puma-like creature had allegedly roamed the Exmoor countryside since some fleeting glimpses in the 1970s. In 1983, it came to national attention after scores of sheep were mauled and killed. There were countless bounty hunts, safaris and expeditions. Even one conducted by Royal Marines. All failed to hunt the beastly thing down. Blurred photographs and a succession of intriguing sightings followed, including one by Lew Pluck, a Dunster chimney sweep who swears he saw a massive pussy-cat with a 'two foot long tail' sunbathing on waste ground behind the Foresters Arms pub. His sighting was reported in the *West Somerset Free Press*. The one near Croyde, however, made the quality nationals. Well, let's just say a reporter from the *Daily Mail* turned up.

With admirable caution, Sergeant Pearce informed the reporter, "It almost definitely looks like it could be the Beast of Exmoor. It's only about five miles away to Exmoor by sea, it could easily have floated down."

"It certainly looks quite beast-like with those teeth," PC Tucker added.

However, the bobbies were proved wrong. Samples sent for analysis revealed that the deceased was simply a grey seal. Decomposition had caused its flippers to vanish, revealing bones that looked like they might have been legs. The Beast was still out there, some would have had you believe.

A closer read of the *County Gazette* left me disappointed. The letter to the paper wasn't about the Beast at all. An owner of a Jaguar car had merely written to complain that he had to get someone to valet his vehicle twice a week due to the mud on Exmoor roads. What did he expect – water hoses at every farm gate and farmers to wipe their cows' backsides with Andrex? Long have the bibblers in the Bear Inn, affectionately known as the 'Bearin' Up', grumbled over their pint glasses that we would soon be told to sweep up the moorland leaves. Like modern loo roll, the world had gone softly moisturised.

Yet that letter highlighted the problems posed by 'furriners' not understanding country ways. Many continue to buy up the local housing stock as second homes in search of the rural idyll they see in romantic TV programming like *The Darling Buds of May* or *Heartbeat*. Then again, I'm where I am because of Laurie Lee, but never found life quite as straightforward as merely having *Cider With Rosie*.

Recently BBC reporter Jon Kay visited the 'jodhpurville' of Exford to see what the full-time residents thought of second homeowners. What struck him was how few of the cottages had lights on or smoke coming out of the chimneys into which jackdaws were moving in. Mark, a twenty-something Exford denizen, called it "a nightmare". The problem has been growing for the past ten years. House prices don't reflect Exmoorian incomes.

Wendy, another resident, was equally critical by saying: "Second home owners are taking the housing that we would like to have available for our locals, but they just out-price us, so our children grow up and can't stay put."

A third resident, Tom, explained the effects of the travesty by saying, "The newsagents has gone, the garage has gone and if a lot of these properties were filled, perhaps these businesses could have been kept going."

Indeed, an estate agent friend confided in me that in one Exmoor house for sale he had twenty-five prospective buyers look round the property and not one of them was a local resident. Scant advice has, however, been proffered by the broadcaster and housing expert Kirstie Allsopp. She maintained the responsibility was on communities to save themselves, but failed to offer any wisdom on how. Current challenges with housing, finding work, rigor mortis at bus stops and a sense of social isolation are causing an Exmoor exodus of young people.

With Bonfire Night come and gone, a helpful youth studying modern history who was a dubious pal of Felix, my rugby playing son, on due cogitation of the housing problem that was affecting himself, flicked his fag lighter and muttered into the flame about Welsh nationalists finding the 'proper solution' for unwanted 'furriners' in cottages. "Be nice," I said, "Big-wigs say grockles and tourism are Exmoor's bread and butter."

"I prefer toast," said the youth.

It must be fellows like him that had caused Ilfracombe rugby club west along the A399 to celebrate Guy Fawkes with a 'non-fire night'. The club had showed footage of a roaring bonfire on a large screen, with speakers playing the sound of crackling wood. The two thousand revellers watching the whizzbang display of fireworks had their cockles warmed by giant heaters. Paul Crabb, the club president, said the quirky idea was adopted, because five qualified fire marshals and metal barricades would have been needed to keep people at a safe distance. Health and safety legislation meant a real bonfire was not financially viable. Asked where the idea for the event came from, Paul said external influences had played a part. "It was lager, probably,' he admitted. 'We were all sat round the table discussing the pros and cons of having a bonfire, when the idea of a virtual fire was thrown into the discussion and everyone thought it was a great idea." Surely they should have stuck to the cider.

Suffice to say without plasma screens and firework dazzle the darkness of

Exmoor's sky achieves wonderment in a stargazer's eyes and country taught lessons become clear. How clever to tell just by looking up at the heavens on a clear winter's night that it was going to be too frosty to plough the fields. The 'handle' of the celestial Plough would be trying to touch the ground with its 'ploughing' bit pointing straight upwards.

And this was how it was when my friend Ray and I had headed home on a winter's evening with a boot load of line caught hobbit sharks and pollack. As fate would have it the Tom-Tom in Ray's plush new Range Rover had played up and had taken Ray on a detour, as I snoozed. The over engineered lump was static at Sandyway, when Ray shook me awake. "Want to see a geminid shower?" he said excitedly.

I must have looked befuddled and perplexed. "M-e-t-e-o-r-s." Ray said the word slowly in the manner an Englishman might speak to a 'furriner' from far afield. He was as keen an amateur astronomer as he was a fisherman. Never wanting to shirk an opportunity this was a man of telescopes and telescopic rods.

A telescope, as big as a bazooka but a tad more constructive, was already set upon tripod at the roadside and pointing at the fundament, that's to say Space, not Ray's buttocks.

"Look over just up and to the left of Orion's shoulder. That's his right shoulder, if he were looking at us," a said Ray.

"You what?" I said.

Ray showed me. Oh, my word! There was a display that was fit for the gods. I beheld meteors and a fireball. Magnificent wonderfulness.

I understood Exmoor National Park Authority was hoping to become the first English National Park to achieve Dark Sky Park status. I mean to say, Scotland now had one with Galloway Forest Park, so it's only fair we should have had a go. Apart from Galloway there are only three other Dark Sky Parks in the world, all of them in the U.S.A. - Natural Bridges National Monument, Utah; Cherry Springs State Park, Pennsylvania; and Geauga Park, Ohio. They are simply areas that have been recognised for their lack of light pollution at night. So, remove a few fuses from the fun fair electrics at Butlins and things would be fine and dandy. As I've said before, Exmoor's been the Darkness to me ever since I discovered its general lack of street lighting.

Exmoor's bid came 2009 during the International Year of Astronomy and was marked by an organised event called *Heaven's Above* in held at Porlock Village Hall. Here the adventurous could handle real meteorites and make a rocket, something that to my untutored self sounded a bit dangerous. But then Emma Dennis, Exmoor National Park Authority's landscape officer, asserted: "There's a tremendous amount of work involved in applying for Dark Sky Park status."

She added, "We would very much like to try and raise funds for a good tele-scope that could be used for educational purposes." I don't think she meant spying on gravity defying swine, or for that matter, the orange clouds that seem to hang more frequently above Welsh industry across the Severn Sea.

To give credit where credit's due, Exmoor is one of the few areas in Britain with skies dark enough to enjoy viewing the night sky. Such skies are rapidly disappearing and less than ten per cent of people in Britain can now see the Milky Way from where they live.

To achieve such elevated status lighting experts would have to be brought in to ensure the night skies above Exmoor were indeed pitch black. This would be done with the aid a sky quality meter that measures the darkness of the sky overhead. A rating would be given. The higher the sky quality meter reading the better the conditions for viewing stars, with the darkest reading, such as would be recorded in a photographer's dark room, rated 24. Out of interest Galloway got a rating of 23.

Not everybody is happy about the state of affairs as letters sent to the *West Somerset Free Press* proved. However, another of Exmoor's Dark Sky organ-isers went on record insisting the hoped for award would boost tourism. Defi-nitely the good folk of Exford should be consulted. Encouraging the 'furriner' to sightsee seems a one trick pony. The worry must be that an influx of tele-scopes coincides with more empty houses with chimney nesting jackdaws.

Tim Bonner, of rural pressure group the Countryside Alliance, recently voiced his concerns. "Allowing small-scale sustainable development", he said, "would protect services such as post offices, shops and doctors surgeries in villages. There need to be homes and opportunities for jobs. If we don't address these problems, we have the threat of ghettoisation of the country-side, where only rich people can live there. That would be a desperately sad thing."

Certainly, something needs to be done now that growing numbers of disenchanted locals have started to experiment, adding to the statistics showing increases in rural drug use. It's a problem with potentially serious implications.

I cite what may only be a wicked rumour from an anonymous source on the Exmoor fringe. There had been much giggling in a newish factory making 'Jesus nuts' for military helicopters - the nuts being important items to keep rotor blades attached to body and soul. Lads of the nightshift took loo breaks to get as high as Pluto on ketamine inhaled incognito behind welding masks - a pastime my source rigorously denies partaking of. Although on the World Health Organization's 'Essential Drugs List', I'm sure the listing is for ketamine's core medicinal properties, not for it having side effects that put it on a par with marijuana.

But as far as Tim Bonner's comments go, perhaps he's just expresses my own innermost fears arising out of a chap with a valeted beast of a jaguar.

SIX

A New Fangled Yule

'Christmas waves a magic wand over this world, and behold, everything is softer and more beautiful.'

Norman Vincent Peale.

Poet laureate Carol Ann Duffy had written a poem beginning: "On the first day of Christmas, a buzzard on a branch." The days were falling in alarmingly. Norwegian pines trembled in the wind. And despite Brian Seward having given up offering to roast the festive birds of Bamptonians in his Spar bread ovens, turkeys had an inexplicable sense of foreboding.

For the Roadwater Players rehearsals were reaching a frenzied climax in the close confines of their very small stage in the Village Hall. The kind hearts 'that do' added the last stitches to exotic costumes and the final brush strokes of paint to the slow drying *Aladdin* pantomime scenery. Fingers would remain crossed until opening night over Mr Passmore's special effects.

Soon letterboxes would be crammed with many an envelope and Exmoor's postmen would begin to whinge at gathering their weight in parcels, some of which would be stuck with a 56p Christmas stamp bearing a local image.

St Michael's church on Minehead's North Hill had made the news. Instead of local tourism blurbs banging on about the church's turret window, from which a helpful beacon light once shone to assist Bristol Channel sailors, there could now be boasts about another window. A detail depicting Joseph in one of the stained glass windows made by the prolific nineteenth century artist and designer Henry Holiday had been chosen by the Royal Mail to star in its 2009 nativity set. The vicar revealed to the press that he had known the window would be featured for some time, but had been sworn to secrecy.

Elsewhere, the Barle Singers had cleared their collective throats for the forthcoming annual concert in Simonsbath church. Heather and Lois, the ladies of *The Larder*, Wiveliscombe's foodie shop, were also singing fortissimo.

"What a delightful sound!" I called out whilst deciding between green bean or carrot and chilli chutney to go with the warm bread, slab of tasty cheddar and small bottle of elderberry and port liqueur already in my hands.

"A good sing-song makes us feel Christmassy," said Lois, beaming.

"Keeps us sane more like," said Heather applying order to top shelf chaos before descending the stepladder to answer a ringing telephone. "Oh, hi Andy … Ah … Why are you pissed off? … Oh, you can hear us through the ceiling."

But you can't keep a good tune down. I 'pa-rum-a-pum-pummed' discreetly to myself down the hill and alley steps until I reached my warped blue front door. A gentle man who resembled a cross between a fatigued wing-commander and a weary-eyed Bohemian in a crumpled sports jacket was waiting for me. Patrick, inventor, sculptor and collector of Bakelite plastic to the point of renting old wood-wormed local mill barns to display the stuff, looked like a chap who wanted to talk. Although well known in certain media circles, he lived mainly by takings from his museum's honesty box. Unfortunately, honest punters were few and his overheads large. I often empathised with Patrick that modern life was difficult to manage. His beleaguered expression caused me to think he wanted to discuss the point further.

"I'm traumatized. I blame the BBC," he said. "They invited me to Bristol to talk on the radio about Bakelite. Of course I went, but because they don't pay expenses I left the van in Wellington and went by bus. I don't know Wellington and I don't know about buses."

"Fancy a cup of tea? Earl Grey?"

As we hugged our mugs and brew slurped, Patrick explained his ordeal.

"I got back to Wellington and just wanted to get off the bus, but didn't know where the bus stop was, so I stood up. The bus driver shouted, 'Sit down!' at me. That set off the passengers. 'Ring the bell!' they yelled before a large brute with forearms of tattoos, sat a few seats behind me, growled, 'Yer mate, ring the bell. 'Ere, don't I know you?'

'No.'

'Oh, I think I do. You live local.'

'Actually, no.'

'I think you do.'

Then they all began yelling again 'Ring the bell!' like a damn pack mentality. So I panicked and rang the bell, but it was in the wrong place. I had to sit down again for another mile. Nasty experience. Made me feel very uncomfortable. Trouble is, there're never any Exmoor buses to practice on."

"Well, should you find one, try Missus Tudball's Dictum."

"What's that?"

"Tell the bus driver you want two returns. He'll say: 'Where to?' You say: 'Back yer, you girt vule.' Anyway, if you want to go to Dunster by Candlelight this year, you'd have to go by bus. Car parking's been banned. How about a cheese ploughman's with carrot and chilli chutney?"

Patrick perked up. "Oh, guess, what? I'm being fed again tomorrow. My friend Otto's got me a job at Butlins."

"At Butlins?"

"Yes. I'm helping put up the staging for the big *Nightmare before Xmas* event. I have to wear yellow hard hat, a totally new experience. And there's a promise of a free ticket and cafeteria hot meal. How could I say no?"

Certainly, Butlins themed weekend events added a 'je ne sais quois' to the Friday evening aisles of Minehead's Tesco. Whether it was hordes of indie kids, girls in cowboy hats or '60s retros wearing beads, all bought crisps and cans of beer on route, prior to entrapment behind the entertainment camp's gates. The partying masses contributed nothing to the town's economy.

The event for which Patrick might hold a precious ticket, my clued-up teenage son illuminated me, was really a music festival which the majority of our population has no idea exists. Involving forty or so bands it was organised by All Tomorrow's Parties or ATP. *My Bloody Valentine*, an '80s formed, shoegazing Dublin band was headlining.

I was astounded that not only was Butlins was expecting a crowd of about six thousand to watch a band standing almost still, gazing at their shoes in a detached introspective way playing distorted rhythm guitars and shatteringly loud, droning 'neo-psychedelia', but that youth were encouraged to don smoking jackets and ties.

If my research serves me well, then a certain type of clientele is drawn to ATP. Each group of festival-goers apparently includes three malnourished male art rock nerds and one female with a Karen O haircut which looks like a large flowerpot's been bonce-plonked and cut around. The groupings were as they were because the Butlin's chalet rooms slept four. So it was a lad and his girlfriend, the lad's best mate and the sad 'who-can-we-put-up-with' soul. At least three of these people will be in a band themselves or involved in a "musical project". And jazz loving sophisticate Patrick was getting a ticket? Although I wasn't sure if he had a smoking jacket, he did have a de-mob suit. Perhaps that would be fitting.

Unbeknown to the music lovers, down the road in Minehead town square, a rival nightmare had occurred. The snow-making machine, drafted in to give newfangled romance to the switch-on of Minehead's festive lights, couldn't be used. Unseasonable heavy rain and gale force winds had put paid to it. The local chamber of trade chairman Marcus Kravis, who, according to the *West Somerset Free Press*, spent the evening in the town hall ensuring the streets resounded with Christmas songs, said the event could not have been better. The paper further reported that 'pop heartthrob' Jimmy Constable, from a boy band with the unfortunate name of *911*, flicked the switch to give the town 'seasonal twinkle.'

Twenty-four hours later the elements still hadn't relented and Dunster, too, got a drenching, quite affecting its candlelight. Water dripped from my nose and down the back of my neck as I sought to catch up with friends. Despite the weather flickering candles were everywhere: in windows, in jars on the edge of streets and in lanterns. Lustily singing carolers squinted at their verse sheets charging an atmosphere harkening back to golden age of Christmas. Not as far back, mind, as the cradle of our desert religion, but to the Victorian as shops tried to boost their trade in the recession. Everywhere was nostalgia and the decorated. Everywhere there was colour, bustle and rummage. Mistletoe hung in porches dripped rain drops in the drizzle.

A handle-turning barrel-organ player sported a bowler-hat, whiskery side-burns and endlessly grinned a gap-toothed smile. A jester of a juggler did his best with slippery batons. Old ladies laughed with Santa, reminding him about when they were slips of girls and of wish lists unheeded for decades. Young couples snogged. The furtive smoked illicit substances in dark nooks, given away by the glow of ash and that certain distinguishing smell.

Of my friends, Neil, wearing stockings and a tricorn hat, stoically played the dulcimer with a pair of wooden spoons, while Reg, a bearded I.T. lecturer, had scuttled with hankies and bashing stick, jingling his bells like the rest of his fellow West Somerset Morris Men, to dry out beside the log fire in the pub where Pam the landlady grumbled. She was missing out on what she thought was a rare business opportunity denied to her by the Candlelight Committee, who she claimed wanted an exorbitant amount for her to have a burger stall on the cobbled pavement outside the pub door. Any space had its price that night. Pam's space would have set her back £200.

As for myself, with my jacket collar upturned I was trying to look inconspic-uous in the crowd. Yet I had the paranoid feeling that the stilt walkers, advan-taged by being nearer God, looked down on me thinking, it's him! Dunster in December made me nervous. Skeletons were not just to found in the castle's gatehouse dungeon, they were also in cupboards.

Goodness sake, it was almost the first anniversary of proving the dangers of the darkness. Headlight dazzled, I'd managed to kill my little green car by ever so slowly rolling it over on its roof by the front door of the Luttrell Arms Hotel. I'd broken the steering rack on an ancient Yarn Market stone placed by an idiot. Two of the police closing the road in the face of chaos and a fast gath-ered crowd couldn't help but grin at the voice who called out, "That's that filmmaker bloke who's flat-packed the Peugeot." The bush-telegraph reached Dunster's outer limits by ten, and Dunkery and East Anstey by midnight.

Then there was that unfortunate money related incident at the village castle that landed me in Exeter County Court. It was purely a misunderstanding. As a child I'd played happily with my toy cars in the castle's orangery and had the run of the rest of the rooms making echoey 'whaa-whaa-whaa' Red Indian noises whilst my Granny took tea with Lady Luttrell, a very old friend of hers.

By the time I'd grown up and wanted to film an evening's entertainment in the same building as part of a little retail video called *An Exmoor Country Christmas*, the National Trust had gained ownership. The Trust wasn't nearly as permissive as Lady L. In order to film I had to grovel and behave, but at least there were no fees involved.

I arrived in daylight giving myself time to do a small feature about the Leather Gallery that contains a wonderful set of sixteenth century leather wall-hangings, thought to be of French or Flemish origin, depicting Antony's affair with Cleopatra. Here it's said, around Christmas, footsteps of the castle ghost can be heard, albeit Lady L. never heard a thing. This festive spirit, though, was one of a several hauntings about the castle, like a ghostly foot covered in a talc, or some similar looking powder, seen by a work experience lad; a Royalist soldier called Richard; and most recently, a green dressed man in the National Trust's stable block shop who spoils many an item with a sticky brown substance.

As I stomped around the Leather Gallery off-camera, the castle's golden labrador watched me with disapproval. Back on-camera I spoke of the ghost never having been seen by human eyes and that the phenomenon was as yet unexplained. The labrador then eye-balled me with total disdain.

I, however, was blind to the problems to come when, in the great hall with many a stag's head bedecked with tinsel, ribbons and ivy, the evening's guests arrived and I pushed my camera's record button. Neither was anything amiss when the entertainment began with the vicar strumming "Little Donkey' followed by a 'proper speaking' chap reciting the words of Roy Fuller, once of the Law, the Royal Navy and Oxford Professor of Poetry:

"Chewing a choc, mum in a frock watches the clock
Knocking in pans fetching of grans and gathering of clans,
Hissing from tins, sherries and gins, upping of chins,
Corks making pops just a few drops, watering of chops,
All this odd joy, tears at a broken toy,
Just for the birth long ago of a boy."

No, the problems began after that brief picture of Christmas Day when it was the turn of Somerset Symphonia. I know it was a subjective thing, but to make them appear interesting I decided on taking more than one camera angle. Focusing a close-up of a young woman playing a violin for a couple of minutes, I then quietly wandered to one corner of the hall, then to the next, before finishing half way up the seventeenth-century carved elm staircase with its oak scrolls and elm flowers. I little bothered with another violinist, more earnest, with a receding hairline. At the time I thought nothing of it other than everything would come together nicely in the editing. And I just got on recording the other performances to come.

Months later I got a phone call. I'd been summonsed.

I turned up in court carrying a VHS player/monitor combo and an offending tape, other copies of which, I'm chuffed to add, had been selling rather well. My smart suited patron, a young Bright Ember, brought his chequebook - rather a negative move, I thought.

The judge recognised me from a past hearing of a totally different nature. "Alright?" he asked me.

"Yep," I said.

Joining us was the earnest violinist. He wanted money. Quite a lot, to be vague. Not just for himself but for sharing with the whole symphonia. The question was whether the symphonia's appearance on the tape was important enough to the programme segment as a whole to warrant payment. Of course it was, contested the earnest violinist who maintained it was a multi-camera shoot.

At the judge's request I pushed 'play' and the four of us watched the video's castle segment.

"Look, you can see she's not playing the right note. Any real musician could tell you that," I blurted, trying to explain the editing process. The balding chap's icy glare could have frozen Hell over.

And indeed, the case rested on the soundtrack. "The highlight of the evening," spoke the narrator to those with bated breath, "was the internationally famous Laudamus choir." "On Christmas night all Christians sing about the news the angels bring," the massed voices sang.

Judgment made, the judge smiled his benediction. My patron put away his chequebook and sighed his relief.

So it was understandable why I was nervous that rainy Dunster by Candle-light, just in case I was recognised in the crowd. But I needn't have worried. There was a bigger attraction. Out of the sog and the wind-howl came sound of a stag. Hell's teeth, was this the ghost of the deer found in open country in 1903 above Challacombe and killed at the gates of the Castle after being driven twenty miles by the huntsman Robert Sanders with the "effortless superiority of a Balliol man"? Had the deer returned to haunt us? No, I was being silly, that creature of stamina had been a hind.

It was, in fact, Johnny Kingdom showing off his secret stag effect by blowing into a plastic tube.

I shouldn't have been surprised. I'd heard on the grapevine that Johnny had been giving a huge red deer stag, dubbed 'The Emperor', his closest attention. And now it starred in the latest of a long line of Johnny's 'wobble-charm' DVDs. Thought to measure three metres from his hoof to his antler, the animal had already been in the news. Although every effort had been tried to keep the stag's location secret to protect him from hunters, Johnny had stalked him out.

Peter Donnelly, a retired deer manager on Exmoor, had told the BBC it was possible the stag, weighing in at more than one hundred and thirty-six kilos, was the largest wild land animal in Britain. "It's a beautiful, magnificent beast," he said. "They normally don't grow as big as that. But he's had top quality food and a mild habitat. I hope all the trophy hunters leave him alone for him to concentrate on what is most important to him at this time of year, which is having nookie with as many hinds as possible. He will be doing what comes naturally to father a new generation."

A group of bedraggled onlookers found Johnny's stag noises to be the topic of discussion.

"I had a drink with him once, woooo," said a waxed horse coat.

"He's a legend," said a man mountain.

"Great bloke, but mad as a bag of adders," said a flat cap.

By coincidence, a week or so before, my wife had sat opposite Johnny on the train to London. She said he stood out a bit in his camouflage garb and wide brimmed hat stuck with feathers. After a young girl had come and asked him for his autograph my wife eased herself into a conversation. He said he was 'goin' up to the city for a 'publicity affair' and was 'required' to wear his camouflage and hat at all times because 'his bosses said so'. The garb was his uniform of celebrity and a grey bunch of TV people seemed to be earning a good living off him. He though preferred to speak about his fifty-two acre plot of land that was his dream come true - his haven for wildlife. Having worked with Johnny myself in the past I know he's really one of the good guys. I just hoped no poacher bought a DVD copy of 'The Emperor' in his landscape.

I decided to leave Dunster's candlelight to Johnny holding court, preferring instead to seek the next bus out. I needed an early night. On the morrow a publicity affair 'required' me to do a book signing gig under wearying fluorescent tubes in Taunton.

S E V E N

Small Tots and Chestnuts

"The ordinary chestnut can beget a sickly and reluctant laugh, but it takes a horse chestnut to fetch the gorgeous big horse-laugh."
Mark Twain, American humorist and writer, 1835-1910.

Sue, a lady in a grey two-piece, tidying a W.H. Smith bookshelf, appeared to be in charge. I tugged my forelock and introduced my biro. "We had Paddy King-Fretts in here signing a couple of evenings ago," Sue informed. "He did very well with his new book about an octopus. And he had a fountain pen. Do you know him?"

I couldn't deny it.

Now in his seventies Paddy had grown up high on Exmoor in a harsher age, and had filled his head with notions of mystery and romance from a solitary existence spent on pony back. He had taken to writing romantic Exmoor fictions of nineteenth century daring-do for a Mills and Boon fed readership of ladies who lapped up stories involving softly crying curlews, banishment, love and Larkbarrow.

Paddy was also a chap once commissioned into the Devonshire and Dorset regiment who in addition had completed two operational tours with the SAS. And he has the respect of his pal, the frostbitten and resourceful explorer Sir Ranulph Fiennes.

What Sue said was true. Paddy had indeed written about an octopus. Yet it was nothing to do with fanciful trysts or entanglements. Instead, it was a novel account of roughtie-toughtie soldiers blowtorching gonads in the night. The fluttering-hearted ladies that queued by the laden table in W.H.Smiths waiting for Paddy to sign and dedicate book copies might well have been somewhat aghast a while later.

My gig turned out to be an affair my publisher thought fit to let the world know about it afterwards by twittering, which is all new science to me.

For those not in the know, Twitter is a free service that lets you keep in touch with people through the exchange of quick, frequent messages sent more often than not by mobile phone, something I don't possess. However, one can read the stuff on the internet and after a tip off I found the following:

"Chas Wood signing in WHS asked by woman for directions. Told he was a scribbler – 'Are you famous?' 'Let's just say notorious,' he replied."

Outside the warped blue front door and the windows opaque with condensation, the heavens had opened yet again and not for the Christmas angels, and the cat was snoozing on her cushion. Wanting to partake in activity I sent an email to my publishers.

"You didn't mention the tie," I wrote, beginning a game of cyber wiff-waff:

"Tweets have to be no more than 140 characters! – I cut out the bit about you wearing a tie - lacks credibility don't you think?!"

"But, but ... it was my Thai tie - the bright blue one with lots of silver elephants."

"Ah that's different, but Thai Tie Tweets are so yesterday."

"So yesterday? Er, no. My dear chap, it was the day before yesterday. Yesterday was sipping hot sake in the line of duty at Dulverton by Starlight."

It had been a long weekend. Suffice to say Starlight had proved to be most entertaining. Well, certainly for me when I went for a gander in the pre-star early, and perversely dry, afternoon. I acted in the same perverse manner, dropping a coin into the tin of the sixth Rotary Club collector I happened by. A thoughtful little boy who said his name was Rudolph offered a carrot.

Outside the town hall the invited Wivey brass band, with each of its members wearing a white bobbled Santa hat, warmed up its instruments. Only slight interest showed in the face of a Great Dane with a pair of cuddly felt antlers tied to its head. There was no Johnny Kingdom, but Captain Coconut began blowing amazingly large bubbles.

Two mounted police horses standing near the bank scrutinised me with suspicion.

"Don't you normally do football?" I said, looking one of the horses in the eye.

"We do bit of everything, really." The voice came from the steed's officious rider.

"'Cor, this horse is a great ventriloquist," I said to a lady with small child stood beside me.

"Are you the Press?" demanded the policeman.

"Nope, just nosy."

"That's alright then" said the policeman, softening to a smile. His horse, he told me, was called Poncy. The other ridden by his policewoman colleague was Brunel. They were all down from Bristol for the day, and having caused a tailback from Tiverton, had somehow managed to squeeze the horsebox into Dulverton.

As Poncy let off wind I noticed Brunel's ears twitch as the pair of pretty shires towing Santa on a carriage trotted by. The small child then took it upon itself to reach up and poke Brunel's semi-erect todger before bursting into tears. Brunel stayed as silent as Clifton's bridge of suspense.

"It's okay, he's trained. Nothing disturbs him," said the policewoman. Obviously she only had thoughts for the horse. Taking my leave I strolled passed a parked Land Rover with a sticker in its rear window that read, "Thou shalt not fart whilst talking to a police officer", and then proceeded up to the church where there was an interesting pall of smoke.

The smoke came from chestnuts charring on a barbeque grill under the administrations of two pensioner gentlemen outside the church door. Going inside the church I discovered among the pews an awful lot of alcohol. Bottles upon bottles. And it was being raffled. A jostle of parent-tugging children from the ages of primary school upward, hopeful of prizes, clogged the aisles. The children seemed much happier here than searching for sugar mice in shop windows. By now the chestnut smoke had wafted into the nave. Some public-spirited individual in the throng must also have seen or smelled it and rung the Fire Brigade.

What followed is a bit of a blur. Around the corner from the direction of the moor came a Fire Rescue Land Rover, blue light flashing, siren blazing. Finding themselves suddenly in front of an onrushing large red metallic banshee, Poncy and Brunel reared. This spooked Santa's trotting shires into a gallop that more than alarmed the hangers-on and quite spoiled Wivey's band's well-practiced rendition of *Jingle Bells*. Bandmaster, Charlie, with his white beard making him a doppelganger of Santa himself, could only hold his tummy through laughter, barely getting a 'pharp' out of his trumpet.

I needed sustenance. I found it in *Tongdam*, Dulverton's extraordinarily good Thai Restaurant, a meeting place for nostalgic local ex-colonial sorts who reminisce about their memories of Singapore and India when they were young chaps and 'gals'. That afternoon *Tongdam* was open for free snacks, a generous gesture from Robert, the owner whose past family had also tinkered with the world order. One, Basil Silitto Cave, had even gone so far as to cause the shortest war in history that lasted thirty-eight minutes over an impasse about a flag in Zanzibar. It was a family that Robert had sort of distanced himself from.

"Fancy some hot sah-kay," Robert offered, "I owe you a thank you."

It was nice to feel valued. I had gone hunting for the grave of Robert's Great Uncle George who was Chancellor of the Exchequer during the First World War and was someone I had wanted to write about. Robert hadn't a clue where the grave was, but thought that it might be in Somerset. I found the grave in Berrow, took a photograph and later emailed the image to Robert.

However, it wasn't the grave itself that really interested him. Upon the grave had been a posy of flowers of a variety uncommon in this country. The posy had a card attached, hand written by 'Estelle'. Intrigued, Robert had made enquiries. Estelle, it turned out, was a long lost relative with some connection to the Queen of Denmark, lived in Melbourne, climbed mountains in Tibet and was by chance visiting Somerset around the time I ventured by Berrow. She and Robert had subsequently become friends for life.

That tot of hot sake helped the tingle of Christmas surge into my soul, much more than a hummed 'pa-rum-a-pum-pum'. This was a tingle that slowly but surely would soon be felt across the length and breadth of Exmoor.

And so it was. In Dulverton itself the display of birds in the butcher's window was perhaps Exmoor's finest. Professional hands entered the backsides of geese to disembowel. The cold store larder was full to bursting with pheasant, rabbit, and venison. And there was no fear of a turkey shortage. Part-timers are called upon to meet large demand. Matt, a university student down from Oxford, had pulled a muscle handling a thirty kilo bird during his holiday job in a poultry factory out North Molton way. He grumbled over a pint in the Bearin' Up that he had ruled himself out of the 'Firsts', however he was referring to local rugby rather than to any potential academic achievement.

At Sindercombe Farm, where chickens go about their usual business of popping in and out of the stone barns, Shep the border collie was appointed 'turkeydog'. He was given the appointment by his flat-capped, blue over-alled master, John Goscomb. Shep's job was to round up the farm's large numbers of angst ridden white turkeys. Shep would flush out those cowering behind the limited cover like a water butt, oil drum or redundant tractor tyre. To hide was futile. Destiny could not be denied. Shep's friend, a brown patched Jack Russell terrier, second in command, would stand grinning, paws in mud, 'on stag', watchful.

However, at least for Shep, the palaver was a time out from his usual day job of rounding up the mules. Something that was not quite as bizarre at Sinder-combe as you might think. Absolutely not. As well as the obvious horse-donkey affair, a mule is a commercial crossbreed of sheep designed to produce prime lambs for meat. And John's farm was well stocked with mules that were shaggy ewes. It's all a matter of understanding.

At this time, deer in the conifer plantations of Spurway Mill appear perhaps a tad worried as thrushes shift uneasily under a shower of windblown sawdust. Dick Spurway might do more harm to himself. The local landowner was one of long line of Spurways whose family have lived around Oakford for generations. Any source of income was most useful, no matter the dangers. Out with his chainsaw, Dick hobbled as he sought out his best Christmas trees for a little cash in hand. A few years ago he had clumsily lopped off the toes of his left foot - proof that Christmas on Exmoor can be a bit of a drama.

But there are dramas that many flock to witness, especially when the Mummers perform in boozy pub atmospheres, whether at Brendon or Heddons Mouth. Led by Master Mummers, Francis and Barbara Verdigi, a sung verse begins things:

> "With a rink tink tink and a sup more drink
> We'll make the old bell sound
> A merry Christmas to you all
> May happiness abound."

Then it becomes raucous, bloodthirsty stuff starring a motley bunch of characters that include dragon slaying St George, Captain Slasher, a Turkish knight, the King of Egypt and a Doctor. Based on the legend of St George and the Seven Champions of Christendom the story is a simple one. Several men-at-arms challenge St. George to a duel and are subsequently slain. The Doctor enters and demonstrates his skill by resuscitating the dead knights. But really, it's all allegory. The play is a celebration of the death of the year and its resurrection in the spring. Yet necessity can instil a humbug frame of mind.

Ruddy faced, rough handed, Russell left thoughts of Christmas until the last minute, continuing to swear as he repaired stone walls in Wootton Courtenay rain. He was soothed by neither a late flowering pink campion nor by a visiting egret attracted to the Avill, the river that, it's said, part inspired Cecil F. Alexander to pen the hymn *All Things Bright and Beautiful*.

Unlike Russell I try to keep my hands as clean as the Avill's waters. After badly wrapping the bundle of family presents I tapped out a Christmas story of my own just as the ice and snow arrived and the traditional Yule ashen faggot burned in the fireplace of the Luttrell Arms.

The Dulcimer of Luxborough

Happy the man, the pigsies say, who makes fine strings to play. Happy the man the Pigsies say who cries on Christmas Day.

The song-thrush had dropped the seed that had wild grown into the cherry tree. A tree that had become gnarled and old. Leaves lay in a last gathering; fallen shades of scarlet-brown, orange and gold. Silas the Shepherd caressed the grey-brown metal bark with the back of his hand. Then he swung his axe. Later Silas lopped yellow limbs from the ancient shrub of box. The shrub Silas called his flute tree.

The Green Man's daughter, the mischievous carer of the creatures that creep
and crawl, and of those of pad, beak and claw, had turned a blind yet
weeping eye. But, of course, she knew the reason of all things meant to be
when the last oak leaf falls.

Ask anybody and each would say that Silas was a kind man. Different but
kind, with a face lined with wisdom rather than age. Tall and thin Silas lived
in a world of thoughts under a wide-brimmed hat. A world of flocks and
musicmaking.

On those nights of bobbing candles and country carolling Silas would
hummer-hum. Hmmm-err-a-herrrm. Very annoying. Oh yes, when Silas
hummer-hummed the pigsies would cover their ears, and stay inside their
holly-holes and leave solstice earth to Man.

No, hummer-humming wasn't tuneful. Absolutely not. Much more like it to
say that it was a drone. A noise made through clenched teeth like a wheezy
bassoon or a throttled horn. Yet it kept Silas company as he sat beside his
seasoned stack of cherry wood, the grain shot through with the colours of
forest sunlight. And as he sat, he waited for his reason. Because wood so
beautiful had to have a reason.

Whilst Silas waited he knife-whittled boxwood flutes that played sweet
music. Flutes of reverie and spin-dance swirl. Simple toys. Gifts for children
who hiccoughed in merriment and in jollity overdone.

Silas had waited for as long as memory. On each Christmas eve as his sheep
turned to face the East he soft-stroked his sheepdog's head. For each squeak
of a mousey long-tail he dropped crumbs of his home baked bread. Then
quietly hummer-humming the shepherd placed his twig-tied faggot-bundle
of ash sticks upon his hearth fire.

As each twig-bond flame-snapped Silas made his wishes. Every year it had
been the same. He wished to be shown his reason. And he wished so very,
very hard to see an angel, because that's what shepherds saw. His father the
carpenter had told him so. A father who had played the dulcimer with a pair
of wooden spoons.

However Silas had never been shown his reason, least of all an angel. So as
his faggot-bundle became embers he would take up his shepherd's crook and
his flute toys and stroll through the fields towards the shimmer-glow of lights

of Luxborough homes. With a tap and rap and humble tug at the rim of his wide-brimmed hat Silas left his gifts at each and every door closed on a child within. The shepherd would stay his steps. Ear straining. Delaying. Content as distant bells rung out beyond the hour of midnight.

Then the year came year when the Green Man's daughter listened. Listened to wishes. She spun her soft wind-music.

The berry-white mistletoe caught Winter's frosty nip. The fox panted clouds. The wood-mouse and bank-vole were stilled under the ghost flight of owls. Deer became statue-grace amid evergreen needle boughs. Nose between paws the sheepdog whined. Silas cradled the dying lamb. Born too soon. A lamb too weak, too meek. "Become the harp-sound of heaven, my little one" he said. And the shepherd had his reason in the peace of solstice earth.

After the passing of hours Silas thought of the lamb that had died and of the knife he had slipped inside. Carefully so carefully. Cutting away the delicate gut. His work so fine. Smooth. Double-spiral strands tight-stretched and resonant. Sad-plaited shepherd strings.

So knife-whittling turned to hummer-humming. Hummer-humming turned to Silence. Wood with the colours of forest sunlight was carved and notched. The Shape forming. Trapezoid upon three spindle legs. A trinity. Then Silas pegged his shepherd strings and found his father's wooden spoons.

Leaving his flute toys early by closed front doors, not pausing to hear laughter and floating flute tunes, Silas retraced ice-crisp footprints home before his sheep all turned to face the east.

As the flock turned, maybe it was just the blur of starlight seen through eyes moist with joy, but Silas saw his angel as he played the harp-sound of heaven with his father's wooden spoons. And tirelessly, so tirelessly the dulcimer sang for a special child until the song-thrush called "Come out, come out' on Christmas Day.

Once more the flute tunes of children filled the Luxborough air, and the Green Man's daughter knew that Man joined the shepherd's world of wonder under the wide-brimmed hat. And the pigsies? Well, they emerged from their holly-holes mischief bound before Silas should hummer-hum again.

EIGHT

Cider Crocks and Grave Snuffling

"I'll squeeze the cider out of your adam's apple."
Moe Howard, American comedian, 1897 –1975.

As a naïve teenager I had a liking for Carhampton parish. It was full of colourful history. Bats Castle, sitting on the highest point of Gallox Hill, conjured up thoughts of Transylvanian vampires nurtured by late night television offerings of creaky Hammer horror films, Christopher Lee and Peter Cushing et al. You can only imagine my disappointment when I got around to a sightseeing visit to find the castle was just a heather, bracken and grass covered Iron Age hill fort of two stone ramparts and two ditches. Not a sign of vampire or even a pipistrelle could I find. So I made enquiries. The castle, I was told by those who know, was named after a previous owner, a farmer called Mr Bat.

For years the castle has been a local childhood playground. And in 1983 a couple of schoolboys got lucky, unearthing a hoard of eight coins with dates spanning from 102 BC to 350AD. Amongst the find were three silver plated coins that became the subject of an inquest. Were they or were they not treasure trove? To be so, the coins had to be fifty per cent or more made of silver. In the autumn of '86 the answer was, yes. But there was a another that went unanswered: who had lost them? Could it have something to do with a fox?

Arguably, the castle might just as well been called 'Fox's' as it was Bats. Leafing through Robin Bush's book *Somerset: The Complete Guide* I came across the suggestion that Bats may once have been known as the legendary fortress Din Draithou, meaning 'Citadel of the Beaches'. Indeed, the interior covers three and a half acres and evidence of occupation has been found. The place is also associated with 'The Fox', a legendary raider whose real name was Crimthann mac Fidaig. He was a semi-mythological fourth century king of Munster and High King of Ireland who was poisoned by his sister Queen Mongfind, an unpleasant specimen who went on to become a goddess of sorcery.

Some say The Fox was the advance guard, encouraging the Irish to come and stay in considerable numbers. John Leland, Henry VIII's antiquary, observed that the locality, particularly in and around Minehead "is exceeding ful of Irisch menne". However, Dr Duncan Taylor, an historian and economist, has recently put the reason down to something more fishy. The Fox was just a red herring.

In Leland's day all overseas fish imports without exception were from Ireland and many small boats carried cargoes of dry salted and smoked red herring or white herring pickled in barrels. 'At the end of the fifteenth century Minehead was the leading port for handling these imports, not only for Somerset but for the whole of the southwest,' writes Dr Taylor.

But influences went both ways. It's an interesting little detail that even though it died out during the Victorian era, the title Earl of Carhampton was created in the Peerage of Ireland in 1785.

Four hundred years after the demise of 'The Fox' the village suffered death on a major scale. The Anglo-Saxon Chronicles state that in 836 King Egbert fought the crews of thirty-five Viking ships. With the Danes in possession of the battlefield, the Chronicles recount a great slaughter. Carahampton was a bloody place to go. A grave for the many.

However, listening to Kate Rusby's *Here We Come A-Wassailing* booming out my car CD speakers had put me in the right mood by the time I arrived in the village. It was the Saturday closest to the Old Twelfth Night and, having eased my way through the throng, I joined Max, Toby and Sowena, a small gathering of cider crocks, in the corner of the Butcher's Arms bar. The evening promised much excitement. In the pub's orchard ciderous toast would be branch hung for robins in honour of them representing the 'good spirits' of the apple tree, shotguns would be fired into the heavens to scare away spirits of evil and the traditional wassail song would be sung.

The Carhampton wassail affair was started in the 1930s by the Taunton Cider Company. The word wassail itself, however, goes back to the Anglo-Saxons. Frederick Snell seemed adamant that it derived from *Waes-hael*, or 'Health be to you', and "formerly denoted a liquor composed of apples, sugar, and ale which was greatly in request at carousals." He added that the term was pronounced 'wazzayal' in West Somerset dialect and was only heard "in connection with the custom of singing to the trees". An acquaintance of Frederick fancied that partaking in the custom must have been like "assisting at a Druidical function of the dark ages," but such notions surely evaporated when 'a somewhat asthmatic accordion' played as an accompaniment.

Yet, despite the contemporary occasion of arboreal crooning there was only one topic of conversation within my group. It was nothing to do with the notorious manslaughter of the dozy owl, accidentally popped off by shotgun at the apple tree blessing ceremony, while I was filming proceedings in the '90's. No, it was a less mortifying topic that had made Max feel the need to write a letter to the *The Times*.

Indeed, not since 1970 had there been such a village kerfuffle. Back then the local council had engaged itself in a protracted argument over the naming of new housing estate built on land behind the High Street. The name 'Carantoc Place' finally got the nod. It did so in honour of the sixth century Celtic saint who took a crotchety dragon for walkies on a lead contrived from the holy man's stole.

Well that's the story should the late Jack Hurley, a reporter, and later editor at the *West Somerset Free Press* be believed when he described events that followed the saint pitching up upon Blue Anchor's welly sucking mud in search of his lost vividly coloured altar that was given to him by Jesus. On the face of it, losing the thing was quite careless.

However, he did discover the dragon that "came with a great noise, running as a calf to its dam and bowed its head humbly". To be fair, Jack was the source of many a fine news feature, that of legend. And as with all best stories there was a happy ending. Carantoc found his altar being used as a table by King Arthur and the dragon got fed in the king's hall.

Jack believed that Leland was familiar with the story, because his pen recorded Carhampton as being 'Carantoke's Town, where yet is a chapel of this saint'. And while the rectory's foundations were being dug, traces were found of a building. It's only conjecture, but it may have been Carantoc's oratory, a place were secular priests lived together. At the time Robin Bush wrote his book in the mid-1990s archaeological excavation suggested early Christian settlement and burial existed just east of Carhampton. So the conjecture might have right.

Yet the bar corner chat wasn't about redundant history. Nor was it about the recent efficacy of Mr Jack charging £5 for 'alternatives' to sit and make wishes in his fairy ring of fungi. In truth, what was being debated was less about kerfuffle and more about snuffle.

The chat was about Exmoorish events having made it into the national papers, yet again; and it was all because of Geoffrey, a fifty-something 'gone bust' farmer and parish councillor who had made a pig a things. He had moved four pigs into a paddock beside the listed Victorian rebuild of a church the summer before but the land was so badly fenced that they kept escaping. They began breaking out as soon as they were moved into the paddock.

After two of the porcine marauders destroyed crops in an adjacent corn field, the hungry hooligan escapees set their sights on the extensive graveyard. Embarking on series of 'break-ins' they caused a Grade 1 disaster. Being ever food hopeful the pigs desecrated several graves. Geoffrey went AWOL. This was another farmer, like Mr Bat, who might benefit from having a castle, I thought.

Following the news leaking out of the pigs quite spoiling the face of St John the Baptist – the church not the Biblical chap - Max's commendable letter to *The Times* had read: "I don't want to boar people by hogging the comments on this but this really does take the bacon for proving that you reap what you sow. No no no no no yes?" Although he may have been trying to make light of things by imitating the ditherer Jim Trott in the BBC series *The Vicar of Dibley,* Max was stepping on eggshells.

Church-related the Carhampton affair may have been, but in no way was it comedic to the earnest and furious residents. In short, in the words of Helen Duffy, a local pensioner, Geoffrey had allowed his swine to make the graveyard look like "a ploughed field".

"It's heartbreaking," she told *The Times.* "The first time they got in, a group of people managed to get them back into the paddock. But they've just come back, again and again. They've made the most awful mess and it's very upsetting, especially for people with family graves there. One grave, which is only about a year old, has been quite badly churned up. We have a beautiful churchyard, which volunteers help to look after and work very hard to keep looking nice. Something like this is just not acceptable."

Another resident, said of Geoffrey: "He's not a very well-liked man and he has just walked away from this problem with his pigs. He's gone to ground and disappeared, but there's an awful lot of anger towards him because graves are being desecrated. It's been a long-running affair and there's a great deal of upheaval in the village because of it. Everyone is up in arms and the vicar has had a lot of phone calls."

Folk were shouting foul. Several would like to have squeezed the cider out of Geoffrey's Adam's apple. Especially so as the local reverend speaking as vicar and as God's messenger was proving a tad unhelpful by trying to dilute the hysteria with reason and sanity. He said that due to the graveyard's size it was "totally impossible" to keep the pigs out.

"As I understand it," the vicar opined, "under English law the responsibility is on the owner of any land to fence it. In other words, we should fence the churchyard to keep the pigs out, rather than the owner of the pigs being responsible for keeping them in. Carhampton has one of the largest church-yards in Somerset and it would be totally impossible to try and fence it."

And of course there was the additional problem of the large badger sett where the pigs had been getting in.

The brave vicar did try to face up to the snuffling oinkers, but they just laughed at him.

Finally, Carhampton's pigs got a visit from Defra officials who apparently could do nothing either, because Geoffrey was nowhere to be seen. According to residents he lived an itinerant lifestyle and didn't even own a phone.

When it came to calling time on the problem, it proved difficult. The church clock, silent for years, had gone on holiday for an expensive overhaul, removed from its familiar place on the tower by a rope-dangling engineer. He was supervised from furrows below by the onlooking pigs.

However, the saga did come to a boring end.

While a meeting of the local parochial church council decided to 'investigate' fencing the churchyard, Defra animal welfare officers collared Geoffrey and made him agree to keep his offending pigs in a shed.

In our pub corner where we had been cogitating events and quietly bibbling, Sowena said she thought that the pigs were lucky creatures. "Why?" said Toby, "Because they didn't die like Danes?"

"No, 'cos they have thirty-minute orgasms," she said. And with that we went outside so as to not miss the singing of the Wassail Song by a circle of other wobble-legged cider crocks, or indeed the shotgun blasts that met the last hurrah. Not really knowing all the words, I mimed as others sang:

> "Old apple tree, we wassail thee,
> And hoping thou wilt bear
> For the Lord doth know where we shall be
> Till apples come another year.
> For to bear well, and to bear well
> So merry let us be,
> Let every man take off his hat,
> And shout to the old apple tree!
> Old apple tree, we wassail thee,
> And hoping thou wilt bear
> Hatfuls, capfuls and three bushel bagfuls
> And a little heap under the stairs,
> Hip, Hip, Hoorah!"

Hoorah indeed, I thought, the efforts of those delving graveyard pigs would probably have paled into insignificance had the archaeologists arrived seeking out a saint or even a fox. If they had of done, the local themselves might have gone 'Bats'.

NINE

Mixed Bags and Feathered Bombs

"The fascination of shooting as a sport depends almost wholly on whether you are at the right or wrong end of the gun."
P. G. Wodehouse, writer 1881 –1975.

It was a bad time to be game for anything. Preferring against trying to knuckle down to doing a little work to better myself on a day of sporadic and distant bangs, I joined others of similar mindset, Tom, Ken and Phil in the Bearin' Up, the affectionate name used by us and many other a local for Wivey's Bear Inn. I broke in on a conversation about a wedding present for Tom's angelic niece. Whether she should be bought twin beds or a double bed was the conundrum. "I reckon on twin beds," decided Tom. "If the marmalade's on the table you leave it alone. If you have to get up to get it, it tastes delicious."

"I thought, going by the smell, my vest and underpants would taste lovely, too," said Ken. "There was me thinking I was coming downstairs to my good lady frying me bacon and eggs, and what did I find but her drying out my undies under the grill. I went and moaned to Godric."

Once of St John's Ambulance, and accompanied by Godric, Ken had been the giver of First Aid talks to Women's Institute gatherings from Brushford to Brayford. Godric was a skeleton whose bones were held together by metal pins. A WI lady asking the intelligent question how Ken knew that Godric was a 'he' rather than a 'her' was told without hesitation it was definitely a gentleman. "'You can tell by it not having a worn down jawbone," Ken had said.

Godric used to get dressed up in a pair of Ken's cast off gardening trousers, a patched and frayed shirt over the top of which was a grubby overcoat, and a flat cap, and he was left to sit on sunny days in Ken's front porch. When the joke wore thin after some upset Halloween trick-or-treaters whinged to their aggressive parents Godric was relegated to the garden shed. Here Godric was first consoled and then chatted to for hours on end by Ken's six-year-old daughter. Ken was in little doubt she thought the skeleton lonely. And his daughter's habit of collecting chicken bones and metal tap parts in a box under her bed was possibly explained by some secret hope in the future of Godric having a friend made.

I chipped in that our mutual friend Mooseman had zoomed in on Google Earth to discover a donkey bizarrely standing outside Wivey's *White Hart Hotel* and rather than consider what the beast was doing he had pondered, given the Dunster Country Fair started out as a Donkey Derby, that Wivey fête had potential. Mooseman was of proven enterprise having bought a piece of steep bluebell woodland for the cost of two second hand cars after some kind soul had pointed out a loophole in the Inheritance Tax laws.

After some thought Ken believed Mooseman's donkey must have been cold calling in search of a roofing job like the one given to another of its kind known as 'Zulu' that carried timbers from Porlock to Stoke Pero church betwixt and between Horner Wood and the heather splendour of Embercombe. But that was in a different economic climate. Now such work would probably go to neighbourly Eastern Europeans.

As we bibbled and bantered lost in our world of hair and hooves, Tom, a failed gamekeeper-cum-nature lover confessed to having been unlucky in his £400 choice from the litter. Tig, a cute black labrador puppy lay at his feet with a countenance of profuse apology taking comfort in a chewed, slobbered over, soft toy pheasant from Mole Valley Farmers. She was being 'trained up' by Tom as a gun dog and her first outing had not been encouraging.

That morning the other seven dogs, labradors and spaniels, had behaved impeccably. Stood alert at their master heels at the top of the field facing the wood, they had waited, bodies tense, poised, fetch-ready, for when the gun salvos met the overhead whirr and clatter of pheasants. Not Tig. Deserting Tom, she had disappeared to the field bottom that ran along beside the main road, in pursuit of a wind-blown blue plastic bag that she intended to snuff the very life out of by a feat of wanton destruction. And in that she had done a magnificent job. With wagging tail Tig had carried a shred of evidence proudly back to post. It pained Tom that a mate on a tractor and several passing locals from their cars had borne witness to his pup's achievement, not to mention his ribbing fellows with guns.

"There used to be some big guns on *Exmoor*," said Phil dreamily into his pint of Tawny ale.

"Used to be?" I said jumping to the conclusion that the 'big gun' of a music mogul in the vast, tree hidden edifice behind Phil's had perhaps decided to sell-up and move to quieter climes due to the antics of Phil's dreadlocked son, Roger. The influential chap, who managed famous celebs of the ilk of Phil Collins, had only moved in a few months previously. Roger, with his routine gun practices, must have irrevocably shattered any hope of rural tranquillity. It was quite possible. Those incessant daytime volleys of shot blasted at semi-domestic pigeons and pheasants, and those triggered off nightly at fox and sprunching bunnies during wheel-spinning, night lamping through the wound-down window of a mud-spattered, much dented Fiesta, can't have been kind on refined ears. Then again, it couldn't have been Roger's fault. He was on his gap year in charge of a herd of horses in New Zealand.

I also doubted Phil was referring to the former gamekeeper into heraldry now living in Minehead who had held sway over 'ten million acres of Kenya', had come to Exmoor via the Australian outback, had claimed to have seen Lord Lucan, and whose petite, chain smoking wife swore like a trooper and had a penchant for mustard coloured corduroys and waistcoats. No, despite the rare couple being in danger of shooting anything that moved, Phil couldn't have been referring to them as they hadn't gone anywhere other than to guddle at their pub of preference. So, what was Phil on about?

"Four four-inch anti-aircraft guns, one two-pounder gun and two twenty-millimetre anti-aircraft guns," said Phil.

"Bloomin' 'eck, Phillip, them fezzies and partridge are in for a hard time," laughed Ken. "Mind you they'd be great to see off feathered exocets. Remember Molland?"

We all did. Molland's feathered bomb from the Kamikaze Section of the Game Bird Resistance Movement had entered the Exmoor folklore of giggles. It had been a stunning display from a member of the failed guardians of Molland Common's rumoured black grouse - a bird whose numbers had declined across Exmoor from thousands in the eighteenth century to oblivion with 'disturbance' cited as a major cause. Indeed, the last official sighting was a female at Lucott Moor in dimpsey light during the autumn of 1981 pestered to pass the mantle of up-market popularity to the red grouse instead. This really wasn't a good idea. In 2002 the whole red population was thought to have joined the black in grouse Heaven. However, despite reports to the contrary reds still hang on in there somewhere in the Dunkery vicinity thanks to the noble efforts of a shoot.

Anyway, the press had jumped at the story of a shooting party beater being air ambulanced and hospitalised after being knocked out cold by a small one-and-a-half pound Molland partridge. Grousing aside, with up to three hundred partridges bagged in any one shoot retaliation wasn't really surprising.

Ian White, an Oakford chap in his early forties, was beating for a group of eight shooters at a shoot arranged by gun manufacturers Holland and Holland on the Molland Estate. As he was being driven slowly at about 15mph in the back of a pick-up truck the partridge gave its life by flying out of a hedge to thump into the side of his head. There was talk of getting the brave bird stuffed but Ian honestly didn't want to see it again. He told a reporter that it was lucky the bird wasn't a four-pound pheasant. "If it had been a bigger bird, then I probably wouldn't be here today," he grimaced.

News of such misadventure had turned a few folk, Phil included, toward the relative safety of potting at clay frisbees. Unfortunately, Phil and guns didn't quite go together. Even his popping at rats with a two-two air rifle had given way to him graciously leaving them to his efficient cat, Harpy. And his confidence took a further dive one afternoon when he felt abundant with grit and stoic determination he normally reserved for the cricket field: "Pull!' ... Floooump went the trap ... Bang! ..."Bother!" ... "Pull"... Floooump ... Bang! ... "Bother!" ... And so it went with little change until by the law of average Phil finally exclaimed, "Ooh, ooh, hit a bugger!"

With the event common knowledge Ken wanted Phil to elucidate on the pronouncement of potentially new firepower. "Not planning on taking anti-aircraft guns to your clays are you, Phil?"

"HMS *Exmoor*, the ship," said Phil. "A British Hunt Class destroyer sunk by either a German E-boat or a mine in 1941. She was only a year old. I was reading up about her. Her badge sounded lovely, on a red field there were two foxes brushes in Saltire between two mullets gold. It was so ... Exmoor." He was right, of course. I recalled how John, a former publican at the Exeter

Inn just outside Bampton liked to shoot a fox before breakfast each morning and handed out fox brushes to children as they waited for the school bus. A few years later those self-same tails would end up hanging cherished from rear view mirrors in cars held together by 'bits of string'. John's specials blackboard menu would regularly offer 'Local mullet' and 'Rat' - the latter saving him the trouble of spelling 'ratatouille' for the vegetarians.

And only a short while ago, Phil had had the foxhounds through his barns. He wasn't sure which foxhounds, or whether they were really allowed to be there given left wing Westminster meddling, only that the chap in red on the horse seemed very pleasant almost apologetic: "So sorry to disturb but do you mind if my hounds have a sniff around your barns, they're on the scent, you see." The chap was careful not to say what the scent was of, but not wanting to be too distracted from making a holly wood case for a grandfather clock for a paying customer, and having recently lost a couple of good laying hens and with his son being otherwise indisposed, Phil told the foxhounds they were most welcome.

As a boat builder turned carpenter, Phil loved his naval history from all eras. Indeed, he was an avid reader of Patrick O'Brian the creator of the Aubrey–Maturin series of novels set in the Royal Navy during the Napoleonic Wars on which Peter Weir based his 2003 film, *Master and Commander: The Far Side of the World.* Phil could empathise with O'Brian, a civil man with a philosophy dear to Phil's heart. When not writing about boats and battles, O'Brian immersed himself in fishing, bird watching and country pursuits.

And to tell the truth it was all becoming a bit of a battle out there on all fronts. I thought this upon seeing Jim Webber, a National Park ranger, emerge armed with a flame thrower through the dense smoke that drifted over a patch of tree sprinkled moor he'd been swaling. From somewhere a red grouse might have shouted 'gobak-gobak' to its few remaining comrades, probably unaware that Jim was really as much their friend as the controlled burning was to their benefit. Alastair Balmain, Deputy Editor of *Shooting Times*, commented: "While it may look wild, natural and free, it isn't. Our upland areas are amongst the most intensively managed landscapes around …" Aware the grouse was very demanding, proponents of shooting claim that their activities help the environment. In deference to the men with guns, the enemies of the wonderfully named *Lagopus lagopus scoticus* belonged to science, and particularly from within Cranfield University where grouse were being held responsible for global warming not to mention beetle infestations. 'Kok-kok-kok,' say the red grouse now having RSPB Amber Conservation Status.

Really it was all the fault of moorland burning. It's happening throughout our Sceptred Isle, boffins maintain, on an industrial scale equivalent to a tenth of British total output emissions. Coinciding with the 'glorious 12ᵗʰ' in 2006 Adrian Yallop, an ecologist at the University wrote in the *New Scientist*: "In terms of carbon storage the moors can be thought of as Britain's rainforests. Where burning occurs, the hydrology changes and the peat is open to decomposition and erosion. This strips the moor of carbon as surely as setting fire to the Amazon forest."

And evidence from a 2008 survey caused Bea Davis, the farming and wildlife officer at Exmoor National Park Authority, to comment: "Climate change is beginning to have an effect on the distribution of species".

If this wasn't enough of a quandary there have been complaints in the shooting press of an infestation of the heather beetle, together with calls for public funding to remedy it. Yours and the grouse's fault shout the boffins. Exmoor's intensively managed landscape is an ideal breeding ground for the beetle. Once hatched, they eat the young heather shoots and damage the stems, causing the heather to wither and die. The speed with which they can destroy heather coated areas of is a concern to everyone.

Back in the Bearin' Up conscience dictated Tom, Ken, Phil and I should do something sporting to help the local economy. As Tig gave a pitiful whine perhaps wishing nothing other than to be forgiven or maybe from worry about feathered bombs, we ordered four tots before taking our leave knowing full well that the life of 'the famous grouse' is a short one.

As for Phil, he made it his task to research the firepower of HMS *Exmoor 2*, a Hunt-Class Escort Destroyer that was launched on 12th March 1941 originally as HMS *Burton* after a Derbyshire foxhunt. Following a successful 'Warship Week' National Savings campaign in March 1942, *Exmoor 2* was adopted by the civil community of Minehead. It was a somewhat debatable choice - the foxhunting Minehead Harriers hadn't caught much in living memory. Ironically, she was sold off as useless in the end to those old marauders of the Exmoor coast, the Danes.

As Phil went one way I went the other, scampering home to seek out an itinerant donkey on Google Earth.

TEN

Heavy Heads and Dog Collars

"In the cave of intuitive wisdom I sit, absorbed in the silent trance of the Primal Void. I have obtained my seat in the heavens."
Guru Granth Sahib, Holy Scripture of the Sikhs.

Outside the warped blue front door the collared-doves visited the bird table singularly rather than as a couple. This either meant divorce or eggs. A yaffle echoed a laughing 'ha-ha-ha-ha', while a pied woodpecker scolded 'quick quick' to the early rising spiders on the wall moss hugging hawthorn about to be gobbled by the titty-todger. Bilbo the cat was not quite her usual assertive self with Peckal the tame hen blackbird. And she'd been pooping upon our soft comfy chair, newish carpet and other such sanctified places. Too early for catnip, Gill and Jeremy, the neighbours, suggested it was contact with lily pollen in their garden.

I thought the fencepost caterwauling was merely attention seeking. It was certainly louder than usual. So she may have had a sore tummy and wanted to share that fact with the rest of us that she was regretting a bitter patio-consumed vole.

Six wooden crosses, one behind the other, each honoured with wreaths and weak sunshine had appeared in the churchyard over a space of time too short for the arranged headstones to be erected. Such things were proof of a clink-erbell sharp winter not quite over.

Poppy the Jack Russell had done her best to topple into the berrin awaiting green baize lined grave pit as a mordant organ fugue drifted from the church. Her owner, ex- Royal Navy, was extorting 'Oh, hell, oh hell, oh hell'. Extendable leads were problematic, a profound irritation.

The National Trust reported that spring flowers had been set back by up to four weeks compared with recent years, although they expected that when some decent warmth arrives it could unleash a huge burst of flowering.

Well, certainly the snowdrops were late. Those that grew to make the sign of the cross in St John's churchyard at Cutcombe were less visited than the abundance down the lane beside the Avill. But at least, said many a local, the church specimens followed traditional values of being free to view.

With the motorist having become persona non grata for the season, those resilient to blisters and leg cramps donned wellies or hiking boots and strolled down the Coleridge Way to their goal, the captivating Snowdrop Valley. Whereas the walk-shy, pocket-rummaging, money-grumblers waited beside the new bus shelter in Wheddon Cross.

Costly pint-sized buses collected and ferried down to North Hawkwell Wood. The money taken as fares went to the local school, the pre-school, the village hall and the church.

The owner of North Hawkwell wood, the Badgworthy Land Company, asked for nothing other than the public should refrain from picking the flowers.

Formed in 1926, the company shares are owned by the charitable Badgworthy Trust for the Preservation of Exmoor. By owning more or less seven thousand acres, the company is the largest private landowner within the Exmoor National Park. To quote written evidence submitted in 2000 to the Committee of Inquiry into Hunting with Dogs, "the Company was originally set up by a group of landowners and farmers concerned at the loss of habitat and the effect this might have on the red deer herd on Exmoor at a time when 'The Hunting Debate' was first in the public domain." At a time when hunting's become a drag, snowdrops have been added to concerns.

If the shamanic poet Ted Hughes is to be believed with his themes of survival and the mystery and destructiveness of the cosmos, each individual snowdrop flower is a feminine who 'pursues her ends, brutal as the stars of the month, her pale head heavy as metal.' Small wonder they flourish in an Environmentally Sensitive Area.

But heigh ho, spring was definitely beginning to spring. The day before, Gill had planted some garlic and dug the potato bed in readiness. So, she thought, it was bound to snow again soon.

If her words were to prove reliably prophetic I decided to use the weather window and enjoy a change of scenery. It was time to hit the rocks. I was on a mission. During a browse in a second hand bookshop in Perth, the Oz one of all places, I had picked out a musty hardback that I felt sorry for as it was more battered and ant eaten than its shelf mates. Published in the 1950s and written by Joyce Reason, an author I hadn't heard of, the book was called *Bishop Jim*. Thinking it might have been some sort of sequel to Kingsley Amis's *Lucky Jim*, I began at the end and flicked through a few yellowed pages. A faded sepia photograph showed a frowning, bushy-bearded, dog-collared gent with receding hair gazing with a determined expression and gimlet eye at something to his right.

I soon got the impression that Bishop Jim, whose full name was James Hannington, a Sussex-born fellow, hadn't been lucky. Neither was I. My hands started to itch. Dust mites. Then, halfway down a particularly scratch-inducing page, I read the words 'Martinhoe' and 'Exmoor'. Blimey, this was irresistible. For a couple of Australian dollars the health hazard became mine.

Miss Reason, I later discovered, had been an Essex girl prolific in penning popular missionary biographies. Curious to see where such zealous tendencies began for Bishop Jim I did some detective work and discovered the good man had kept a journal. I had had to go and see what inspired its writing. I took my stills camera, just in case.

Horned shaggy sheep daubed with orange splodges stood out fetchingly amongst brown heather and reed grass. Chewing whatever it was they had a liking for, the sheep gawped at me as I pootled across the Chains. Under scudding grey clouds Exmoor had been left with tiger stripes from the thawing snows of the previous month and the wind was biting. Martinhoe is one of the places that in winter especially there had to be a purpose for going.

Opposite St Martin's church, and sat above a bank of grass, ivy and harts-tongue fern, was Hannington Hall. It was nothing grand, just a newly painted

1930s' rendered brick common-a-garden village hall with a slate roof gathering moss. A poster still advertised: "Christmas Whist Drive. Poultry and many other Prizes. All proceeds to Hall Funds". However, an inscribed plaque on the outside wall was interesting:

"TO THE GLORY OF GOD
AND IN MEMORY OF THE RIGHT REV..
BISHOP JAMES HANNINGTON
BORN SEPT. 3RD 1847
ORDAINED TO A CURACY IN THIS PARISH
MARCH 1ST 1874
CONSECRATED 1ST BISHOP OF EASTERN
EQUATORIAL AFRICA JUNE 24TH 1884
MURDERED BY ORDER OF MWANGA KABAKA
KING OF UGANDA OCTOBER 29TH 1885
BURIED AT ST. PAUL'S CATHEDRAL KAMPALA
UGANDA DEC. 31ST 1892."

There on a stone laid in 1933 was a man's life in a nutshell. Martinhoe was obviously very proud of their Bishop Jim. But, probably due to lack of space, stuff about his local antics had gone unchiseled. As a child he'd blown off his left thumb trying to steal a wasp's nest with his friend, Joe. They had got hold of a broken powder-flask and had initiated themselves into the mystery of making damp gunpowder squibs, or 'blue devils'. He wrote graphically of the mishap:

"The blue devils were in a state of readiness; but we must needs, before starting, try one with touch-paper. The result was not so satisfactory as we had expected, and Joe Simmons says I tried to pour a little powder on the top of it. The spring of the flask was broken, and in an instant a terrific explosion took place. The flask was blown to atoms, and I was to be seen skipping about, shaking my hand as if twenty wasps were settling on it. Simmons senior rushed up at the report, and binding up my hand in his handkerchief, led me off to the house, about a quarter of a mile distant, my hand all the while streaming with blood, so as to leave a long red streak in the road.

"When I reached the garden I was so faint that Miles, the gardener, took me up and carried me. The first person I met was my mother. She at once saw that something was wrong, and, in spite of my saying that I had only cut my finger a little, she sent off for the doctor. I was soon under chloroform, and my thumb was amputated. It was quite shattered, and only hanging by the skin.

I was very prostrate from the great loss of blood, but, through the mercy of God, I soon got well again. I never suffered with the lost thumb, I may say, at all. I used to feel the cold in it; but that also has passed away, although even now I cannot bear a blow upon it without considerable pain. It is a great wonder that I was not taken off by tetanus!"

Such stuff proved Jim hadn't been all there from a young age. To celebrate his seventeenth birthday he shot "eighteen brace of birds, four hares, one landrail. 5 feet 10 inches high, weight 11 stone 6 lb." The latter dimensions I presume referred to Jim himself rather than the bird. By the age of twenty-one, he was at Oxford having decided on a clerical career. In Miss Reason's eyes, he was 'a desultory student' probably due to his admission of "boyish glee in bringing a whole armful of fireworks into college on the 5th of November, and letting them off in defiance of all rules and regulations" or "completing a festivity by galloping round the Quad upon a chair at the head of my companions in riot."

Jim's Oxford college principal strongly recommended his 'Master of the Revels' to seek out a competent tutor where there would be few distractions, and where he would have no temptation to seek other friends than his books. So at a time when Lynmouth became known as Little Switzerland in the eyes of civilised Victorians attracted to the Exmoor Coast by its scenery of water-falls and towering cliffs, Reverend Charles Scriven, Rector of Martinhoe was suggested. And in 1870 Jim duly arrived. The impression he made upon those at the Rectory is recorded in a note: "I found out that their opinion of me is that I am very eccentric."

If the powers that be, thought Martinhoe would sober Jim to a life of reading and botanizing. Wrong. Instead, Jim became a hard rock fan. With the Exmoor coastline offering greater distractions than college life, his climbing and caving adventures earned him the nickname 'Mad Jim'. He had an awful lot of fun before being made a curate, as the plaque said, in 1874.

Turning my back on Hannington Hall, I went to have a look at his old church. St Martin was a fourth century Hungarian martyr, so the church's choice of dedication was probably one of convenience. Despite the Martin family once being locals who owned the parish, the name probably originated from a Saxon called Matta.

I found the churchyard's rickerty double gate latched by a black, buckled strap. I thought this to be a most promising piece of eccentricity. It was matched in the churchyard itself by an out of place brick built oblong topped by a stone slab with inscriptions to the various members of the Crang family, once owners and renovators of Halsway Manor in Crowcombe, now England's National Centre for traditional music, dance and song, and home base for the bell-jingling West Somerset Morris Men.

Shortly before Jim's arrival at Martinhoe Richard Doddridge Blackmore did as I did, and wandered among those gravestones peering at names. Whereas I was merely being inquisitive, he was seeking inspiration for the names of characters for his 'Lorna Doone'. He ignored the Crangs and experienced difficulty in finding a publisher. When the novel was first published in 1869, it was done anonymously in a limited three-volume edition of just five hundred copies, of which only three hundred sold. Republished a year later as an inexpensive single volume, it was a roaring success and has never been out of print since.

Inside, the church was sparsely decorated with little details. A spider plant, or Chlorophytum comosum to the botanist, flourished on a nave windowsill, and a small glass bowl filled with snowdrops decorated a post on the chancel rail. On the wall beside it hung a poem. Called *The Rhyme of St Martin's Church* it was written by someone initialled 'A.H.' and it put the church's past in a nutshell:

"Hard by, the Roman sentry kept
His seaward watch for Celtic horde,
While fitful Devon sunlight gleamed
On heathen spear and sword.

And here through Devon mist and rain
Came godly Christian men unknown
To build a Church in Martinhoe,
To adze the beam and hew the stone.

Small trace the Roman left behind;
But grey St Martin's looks to sea,
Proclaiming on the wind's wild breath
The strong Faith of the Trinity."

The poem's Romans were stationed at a small twenty-four metre square fortlet of three barrack blocks and no officers quarters perched on cliffs over-looking Heddon's Mouth. Perhaps, not being told what to do they whiled away the hours, like Jim, with cliff-hanging games of dare.

St Martin's itself underwent serious renovation during Jim's time. Indeed, he had helped to put in the stained glass east window, having 'recommended Baillie, and obtained the design'. It was a renovation that, for some reason, saw the Saxon font buried out of sight in the rectory garden. However, the font was later unearthed and is now in Parracombe church where locals must think: "What's the Matta with it?"

But of the things still inside St Martin's, the highlight for me lay among the long list of Martinhoe rectors. Above Charles Scriven's name and squidged between '1477 Walter Hendre' and '1488 John More alias Smythe' stood out 'Cornelius – The Irishman'. Bless him. With the Romans gone, a Celt had finally slipped through. And much later so did those of clandestine derring-do. Along with bottles of communion wine the church is rumoured to have stored smuggled spirits. A nose into the parish register reveals an entry going straight to the point: "Dick Jones, died aged 103, last of the smugglers". That was a lot of time to find himself in trouble.

Once in the fresh air again, I wandered around to the back of the church where the Hollow Brook stream flowed on its coarse to become a waterfall over steep cliffs plummeting two hundred and forty metres or more down to Blood Beach. Not being a farmer, lucky for Jim that the local Cow and Calf were no animals. Normally the haunt of gull and kittiwake, and where Fulmer petrels and peregrine took pipits on the wing, Jim found his play-ground.

Today, I understand, climbers from across the land come to the seven-mile stretch of inaccessible coast between Woody Bay and Combe Martin that's known as the Exmoor Traverse. It's nothing to do with the South West coast path and is downright dangerous. Here the brave take on the likes of Cormorant Rock or Scrattling Crack, The Claw or Pharoahs Chimney. Only by being aided by the latest in modern gear can they overcome the problems of access and tidal range.

Jim, however, was the trendsetter, the one to blame, and his legacy is still marked on old ordinance survey maps. With local help he created paths, now sadly all virtually crumbled away, down to the sea. And it all started with a perilous scramble by Jim for some choughs eggs that revealed the existence of some remarkable caves pillared with stalactite, and floored with firm white sand. Jim thought them to be 'the safe and undisturbed citadel of birds'.

He at once resolved that they should be seen and explored. After enlisting servants from the Rectory and some other volunteers for the ridiculous project, he set to work to make a "practicable path" down the face of a dangerous cliff, from nowhere in particular to nobody knew where. Despite at the time being almost incapacitated by a severe attack of shingles, he wrote:

"On Sept. 1st we commenced, and secured two able-bodied men and old Richard Jones to help. When Richard was a boy he had been the best hand in the parish at climbing the 'cleve' (cliff), but now he was old and crippled. We thought, however, he might be useful to do odd jobs, so at 7 a.m. we all turned out with ' pick-isses, 'two-bills,' crowbars, and spades, and made our way to the scene of action."

The enterprise was not without incident. At one point Jim describes hearing the rush of a stone, and a considerable boulder shooting past his head, within a foot of himself. "I had barely time to dodge," he wrote, "as it whizzed by like a cannonball, accompanied by a volley of small stones, and I could feel the draught of air it made."

Understandably, there was much celebration when the dizzy path was completed. An opening day was arranged, and a party of twenty visitors were invited to take some dangerous exercise down to the caves. Jim marked the event with the following entry in his journal:

"Received the Holy Communion with great misgivings. Reflected upon the manner in which I had spent the past year, and made resolutions, which, alas! soon failed."

However, Jim commented not long after: "Took Lord Tenterden, Mr Justice Pollock, and some others to see the caves. They expressed the greatest astonishment at the engineering of the path, and the magnificence of the caves."

The lord and the justice, though, were almost the last to accept one of Jim's invites after a misadventure that still causes Chinese whispers among caving enthusiasts today. This being the case, I shall let Jim tell the story in his own words:

"I asked Morrell and George Scriven, the rector's son, to join in an excursion to a cave we called 'The Eyes', two small holes just large enough to creep through, which penetrated a headland. While there, we discovered below water mark a hole which seemed to penetrate some distance; so, with no little squeezing and pushing, I wound my way in, and found myself in a large hollow chamber with no other outlet than the one I had entered by. It would have been a dreadful place in which to be caught by the tide. The water gradually rising in the utter darkness would drown one like a rat in a trap. I explained all this melodramatically to my companions outside till they grew quite impatient, 'Well, come out then,' said Morrell, ' for the tide is fast coming up, and we shall have a job to return.' So I crawled down to the entrance and essayed to come out head first. I soon stuck fast, and after great squeezing and squirming, barely managed to get back again inside. Next I tried to get out as I came in, and so worked my way down feet first. It was no go, I was again jammed tight. My two friends then got hold of my legs, and pulled and pulled till I thought my legs and body would part company'. Matters really began to look serious. I was bruised and strained a good deal, and escape seemed impossible. And now the full horror of the situation flashed across us all. My mocking words were actually to be realized! I said in the best voice I could that I must say good-bye; but if ever I passed a dreadful moment it was that one. The tide was creeping up slowly but surely. Applying all their strength they pushed me back into the entrance that I might make one more effort head first. Then it suddenly occurred to us all that I might try without my clothes. No sooner said than done; and after a good scraping I soon stood once more by their side. But it was a narrow escape!"

Unsurprisingly, news of Jim's dice with the Grim Reaper soon leaked out and thereafter nobody followed him again down his path. However, of the several caves below Martinhoe, the largest one has now come to be known as Hannington's Cave - an Exmoor legacy for a chap whose life was eventually to end in a tragedy for which there was to be no escape.

Around 1882, upon hearing of the murder of two missionaries on the shores of the Lake Victoria, Jim was motivated to offer himself to the Church Missionary Society. Within a couple of years and having overcome fever and dysentery he was ordained bishop of Eastern Equatorial Africa. Instead of making Exmoor cliff paths he decided, again with the help of a small team but this time of missionaries, to focus on opening a new route to Uganda. His arrival near Lake Victoria did not go unnoticed. Under the orders of King Mwanga II of Buganda, the largest of the traditional kingdoms in present-day Uganda, Jim and the missionaries were imprisoned. After eight days of captivity, the men were killed on the King's orders. As Jim died, his last words to the soldiers who killed him were: "Go, tell Mwanga I have purchased the road to Uganda with my blood."

Having secured the church gate behind me with the eccentric strap, I thought refreshment was called for. Anyway, I needed to warm away the chill of the day. Where better to go than the Hunters Inn, close by down in the Heddon Valley? The lane on the way there took me passed what must surely be the most isolated red telephone box on Exmoor, strategically placed beside an empty grit bin at Mannacott Lane Head.

Like the phone box, the pub sign for the Hunters was also a little incongruous. I could accept a picture of a stag, fox or pheasant, or even a rabbit. But a peacock? This was a new innovation since I last visited the pub to film a band rehearsal for the powerful husky voiced chantreuse Elkie Brooks. She was perfecting numbers like *Pearl's a Singer* and *Lilac Wine* prior to her going on UK tour. At the time she was a local, living with her hubby Trevor and their two sons at Woody Bay, and I was making a video documentary called *Elkie's Westcountry Life*. It was full of behind the scenes stuff like her cooking in the kitchen, walking amidst Exmoor ponies, jetskiing off Lynmouth, looking suitably moody in the Valley of the Rocks or Trevor putting the head of Elkie's pet parrot into his mouth. The video was sold at all the tour gigs. But that was all long ago in the '90s. The last I saw of her was as a photograph on the sun-faded cover of an unsold VHS in a Lynton shop window.

Now, with Elkie and family having upsticked and moved on, the Hunters bar was a filled with quieter tones. Above the hubbub I overheard a couple of lads, one wispy bearded, the other stubbled, talk excitedly about their guts. Judging by the hard hats, ropes and plump rucksacks at their rock-booted feet, I guessed the guts they spoke of were nothing personal, merely the narrow inlets in the cliffs. As chance would have it, they like Miss Reason hailed from Essex, well at least Essex University's Climbing Club if their sweatshirts were anything to go by. They both had a guidebook of some kind in one hand and a half-full pint glass of beer in the other. Interesting, I thought.

"Come far?" I asked as an icebreaker.

"Not really. Just from the old lime-kilns down at the beach. We wanted to try part of the Exmoor Coast Traverse, but it looked too hard," said the wispy beard.

"Have you guys heard of Mad Jim Hannington?"

"Course we have. The bloke was totally cool," said the stubble.

"I think so, too," I said. And finding a common thread we three got talking.

I learned the wispy beard was Keith and the stubble was Kevin, and that they had both intended following cliff-routes made by their climbing heroes, the guidebook writers. Men from the 1950s like, for example, Clement Archer, the chap who christened Blood Beach with its name, and Cecil Agar. Both used extreme methods such as swimming while roped and climbing steep vegetated cliffs with nailed boots, ice axe, home made pitons and secateurs. Alternatively there was free-spirited Cyril Manning, who, during the 1970s was an inspiration to those feeling that climbing methods were being dictated by trendy magazines and equipment manufacturers by climbing solo in big bendy boots. And then, of course, there was Kes Webb who still does the occasional slide show in a village hall.

In 2004 Kes and his wife Liz took part in an ITV production called *The Hidden Edge*. Narrated by Gupworthy resident Simon MacCorkindale and celebrating fifty years of The Exmoor National Park the documentary visited the stretch of the Traverse. At the time it had been explored by only twenty people and those included Clement, Cecil, Cyril and Kes.

One day, Keith and Kevin vowed, they would increase the numbers. At present though they were happy to enjoy the wet rocks and soaking spray around Heddons Mouth.

Outside the scope of their guidebooks I dismissed as anti-grockle waffle the Exmoor legend about a giant crustacean seizing an elderly gentleman by the finger at low tide and holding on fast until the water rose to drown him. Being quite earnest, the lads thought it "a load of cobblers, too, but more a story put out by smugglers to deter prying eyes."

Although, after another half or two, we hedged our bets on the gossip about German U-boats. Their crews are reported to have played night football on the beach with balls made out of rolled up overalls during the Second World War after their vessels had taken on board fresh water by captain's order. Interviewed by a chief *Western Morning News* hack, a Croyde chimney sweep swore by the tale that was told to him by a German in the very bar where the two lads and I bibbled. And the story was now 'out there'.

Surely though, the sweep's tarn was less of a whopper than the 'Gurt Fish of Wringapeak'. This was more of a fisherman's tale with more legs than fins. After surviving centuries it continued to scare the living daylights out of folk.

Heavens, the thing was enjoying as large a life as Jim had once had. When the time came for me to leave Keith and Kevin with their dreams of conquering, I said in years to come I would think of them being somewhere down below as I strolled the coast path.

From behind the warped blue front door that evening I looked back through my photos of the day. One was astonishing. Somehow I had managed to take a picture of a strange orb of light, invisible to my naked eye, floating in St. Martin's nave. I persuaded a couple of photographic 'experts' to have a look. Having scrutinised the image, they independently agreed the orb was no dust particle or reflection of light in the lens. It had to be something supernatural, they said. Perhaps, Mad Jim Hannington' had returned to his haven. Or was it the spirit of Dick Jones?

By the second week of March, with the steel skeletal frame pieces of Cutcombe's long awaited new livestock market being bolted together like an outsized Meccano set to hopefully become an integral part of the farmers role in preserving the landscape, the snowdrop flowers had fully opened. And so had the road down to Hawkwell Wood.

The 'season' was over. With no more micro-buses for another year my wife and I joined the local folk booted and scarved parking their cars down by the Avill in a world that was the galanthus' own. And my camera had another task, a joyous one of capturing a cornucopia of now free Exmoor wonder.

ELEVEN

Fire Brands and Widge Suckers

"Horse sense is the thing a horse has which keeps it from betting on people."
W.C. Fields, American comedian and writer, 1880-1946.

Beside a bare hawthorn tree I crouched in the winter heather on Winsford Hill pointing my rather large camera at some branded, brown and dun, objects of interest. Needing passports by EU directive should they leave the moor, they were fed that time of year by their owners and at other times competed with deer and moorland sheep for fodder.

"What are you doing there? Is it going to be on telly?!" yelled an out-of-season grockle stood within a pack of four across the road from the Latin inscribed Caractacus Stone that, from beneath its little roof, leaned towards the weak sun.

"I'm filming widge beasts and suckers. And more than likely not." I half shouted my reply, trying to make myself heard to folk who appeared to be living life third hand, but not wanting to worry the group of Exmoor ponies and foals. In the latter aim, I unsurprisingly failed. As if to say "What on Earth?" a stallion flung up his head like the Lionel Edwards' cover illustration for that now sanctified book from the late 1950s by Golden Gorse aka Muriel Wace, *Moorland Mousie* - the basis for the Moorland Mousie Trust which funded the Exmoor Pony Centre up the road at Ashwick, a place I had known well. In one of the cottages by the main gate to Ashwick House had lived the dad of Hugh Maynard, the world renowned BBC wildlife filmmaker.

While his dad taught me to drive in a Morris 1100, Hugh inspired me into doing filmmaking of my own. Back then Ashwick House was owned by Sir John Power, a bearded, wiry, liver-knackered guddler of extremes, regularly rescued by his children Alastair and Bindy from a dark cupboard he shared with a fire bucket of sand where he would sing either *The Desert Song* or sea shanties. Some grist I thought for *Exmoor – The Country Magazine* that's recently based itself across the drive from the main house in a building where I had once waited traumatised, intoxicated by booze fumes, awaiting friendly rescue.

On that self same road beside which the yelling grockles stood, following a jerk and a chug at Herne's Barrow my car came to a grinding halt in the dead of night at the supposedly haunted Wambarrows. Both the spider living on a cushion of moss in my wing mirror and I thought: Now what? By happy chance I waved down a weaving car full of good humoured, raucous, reeking guddlers all unrelated to Sir John but who must surely have lived under his influence. I had no other hope than desert the spider.

Even in these days of inventiveness I continue to pootle around this part of Exmoor with trepidation. Knowing mobile phone reception is poor to the point of being nonexistent I try to get back to civilization during daylight as here darkness brings other dangers unrelated to breaking down.

In January 2010 *Horse and Hound* reported the rumpus over the shooting of two eight-month old foals, 'Champ' and 'Bear' on Exmoor Pony Centre land. Police believe they were mistaken for deer and an Exmoor Park ranger conceded there was a problem with poaching. The good news was that Bear survived. However, Champ wasn't so lucky. With a bullet having shattered his shoulder blade he had be put down.

Valerie Sherwin, who ran the centre as well as having a stake in the Exmoor Magazine said: "The ponies were only five hundred yards from my house so someone must have been out with high velocity rifles on private land. We don't believe it was a malicious attack, but it is absolutely disgusting that someone took a pot-shot at them and left them to suffer."

As I tutted and sighed beside the hawthorn tree, the ponies, the descendents of those feral primitives that, if you believe the Roman carvings, once pulled Celtic chariots, wandered off away from me toward Knaplock to grumble about being called by their old name, 'widge beasts'. Until around 1710 there was no such word as 'pony'. Anyway, more to the point, what the hell were those 'grocks' that I wished to confuse doing there this time of year? It wasn't exactly green and pleasant.

While staying at Higher House Farm in Wheddon Cross during his honeymoon Henry Williamson summed things up rather well when he wrote:

"The moor above us is untamed, and black with wind-blasted heather stems. The lower slopes of Dunkery, which is separated from the ancient moor by a hedge of beech, is brown with old bracken as though with the rust of all man's iron machinery which has failed to tame it. The moor seen from the Exford-Minehead road is a black strip, black as a rock spider and as savage. It remains through all the frosts and snows and rains, blasted by the wind and the sun…"

Little change then since 1925, I thought, bearing in mind both landscape and those ponies with their brands. Then again, there was change. Things were going hi-tech as cattle and sheep swallowed their micro-chips. No longer could it be said we were prey to the absurdities of being portrayed as a region of straw chewing yokels. No, we were just being portrayed as gullible chumps. This was something highlighted by the endeavours of Karen Guthrie, a fire-brand of a young Scottish lady artist in residence. Commissioned by a rural project calling itself Triparks set up by Arts Council grant to explore things shared and differing between Exmoor, Dartmoor and Northumberland, Karen had invented an Exmoor National Dress that proved to be quite fancy. And it was something I wouldn't have believed had I not witnessed it with my own eyes.

Karen, her red hair tied in a pony tail and looking suitably smart in pressed hacking jacket and tweed scarf wandered purposefully amid the sheep trailers, cattle trucks and sales pens of Cutcombe market's Exmoor Farmers Livestock auction. She was followed in tow by a not so smart lady attendant with the job of carrying, beneath a protective cover of polythene, an array of creative garments such as a tabard, a cape and a wool woven tunic draped on wooden coat hangers. The attendant also gripped a nine-pointed antler crown made by antlerman Tom Lock in his Hawkridge workshop across the lane from village's central feature of a green painted, long defunct, cast iron, handle-rusted, water pump.

Much time, Karen maintained, had been spent on historic research. To her, the crown represented the traditional farmer's flat cap, despite it probably being more fitting for the common man to have worn a flattened road kill hedgehog as a skull cap, instead. As for the rest of the attire Karen had tracked down other local makers. For example, Maurice Bishop, the well known landscape artist from Dunster contributed the print design of skeletal winter trees for the tabard and farmer-owned Shearwell Data, based at Putham Farm in Wheddon Cross, supplied animal ear tags that Karen had used as costume fixings.

Indeed, the majority of the cattle that careered down ramps off trucks into steel-barred collecting pens edged with galvanised steel crush barriers akin often to those guarding the central reservation of the M5 were possessors of Shearwell stuff. Yes, the beasts had ear tags but they also had a permanent bolus positioned by gravity in their honeycombish second stomach or rectilicum to provide an accurate and effective ID system. Appropriate for both cattle and sheep and taken by mouth using an easy to use applicator, a bolus is no more than a ceramic capsule obtained from a gubbins resistant special mix. Inside the bolus is a transponder sealed in place with special odourless silicon that's immune to an animal's gastric juices. The transponder is marked by a progressive number that can be read by the farmer using a micro-chip reader. Since the very beginning of January 2008 it has been compulsory to have the same responder ID number as the ear tag.

However, there were to be no tags or micro-chips for the Exmoor ponies. Micro-chip readers are only effective at short distances. Consequently the ponies continue to face another fire-brand, a really hot one and this has caused something of a fierce debate.

During a collective branding session at a farm amid pony squeals and the smell of burnt flesh, singed hair, smoke and steam rising from a water butt that cooled the iron, Rex Milton, in red overalls and green wellies and President of Exmoor Pony Society, told BBC News: "Who would like the thought of being branded? It's not particularly nice but it has been proven over the years to be one of the most effective ways to identify ponies. Very often I will get a call about a pony in distress that has been hit by a car on the open moorland. I will ask if they managed to identify it and many people will give me the number which gives us tremendous clues about where to find the pony, what age it is and hopefully we can get on top of the problem very quickly. Believe me when we rounded them up yesterday you wouldn't be getting very close to them with a micro-chip reader."

On the other side of the coin was Ponies 4 People, a volunteer group support-ing and rehabilitating wild and traumatised ponies. Their spokesman Paul King, blameless for the sentiments held in his marshmallow heart, said: "Branding is very painful. It is just barbaric in this day and age for human beings to be doing such terrible things. It is a grotesque thing to do to a pony or any animal to burn it with a hot iron."

Every year Exmoor farmers brand hundreds of foals to act as visible identi-fication and deter thieves. Many of the guys at Cutcombe market agreed that ponies can be very volatile in the wild and until a micro-chip reader is effec-tive at some distance from the ponies, there is no choice but to brand.

I watched Karen eyeing her quarry as rugby-shirted, ruddy-faced with neat sideburns, rough handed Young Farmers, many in baseball caps or those of flat traditional type, tickled and tapped bullock rumps with sticks as others multi-tasked, chomping cheddar and bacon butties while opening and clang-ing shut an array of pen gates.

From a raised box above the auction ring a weathered burly chap of self-import chalked a lot number onto a slate-board on a spindle. He swung it round for all to see as the auctioneer did his stuff of rapid articulation emphasised with hand gestures before banging his gavel with gravitas so securing the four-legged lot to the highest bidder. Karen mingled with the congested crush around the ring that pencil jotted figures onto notepads or perhaps twitched a finger, winked an eye or almost imperceptibly nodded a head in bid.

Karen resorting to persuasive charm soon won herself a victim. "Would you model this for me?" said Karen caressing the crown. "I'd be very pleased if you would. Modelling is the wrong word I know that makes you think, Oh God." And then she laughed.

"You know, I'd be very pleased if you could wear it and these clothes I've made for a photo." In a blink he was wearing the tunic and tabard. "Do you hunt?" she asks placing the cape printed with a Phillip Sanders hunt scene over the victim's shoulders and attaching it around his neck using an ear tag.

"Okay," said Karen turning abruptly business-like. "You'll' probably recognise this. It's quite a traditional. English. Sanders." Maybe it was, but Sanders tended to paint pictures of foxhunts in Kent that weren't quite relevant to Exmoor.

"You look lovely. Now all you need is a crown," said Karen carefully plonking Tom Lock's handiwork on the victim's head. "Quite comfortable isn't it?"

"Look straight into the camera," simpered Karen. Click, click, click went the camera and a minute later Karen was saying: "See ya. Bye."

And for me the jumble of events prompted a tale.

The Prickyback of Hawkridge

Water runs at the bottom but on Hawkridge top there's an old hand pump that gives not a drop. At Hawkridge the sinworms writhed. Where the land steeps away down into the combe of Dane Brook on the one side, and on the other into valley of the River Barle, there once lived an old cross-patch farmer and his labouring friend.

Fustilugs Blowmaunger was surely cow-tongued like his cows. How else could he have spoken fair or foul language to suit his purpose? Smooth one way rough the other that was Fustilugs. From those he asked favours he was a smooth talker. Polite. Always with a promise to pay later. To the frightened-eyed farm animals his words were always foul and nasty. No, Fustilugs wasn't very nice.

The bogles watched that ill-natured man grow fat by full feeding, and they watched him guddle his liquor with his pal Flotch - a man as flabby as a blamange. By night Fustilugs's windows bled both candlelight and the ugly laughter of the beastly drunk.

Matters became worse and worse. The fatter Fustilugs got the bonier his cows became. There was a reason for it. Fustilugs had money but he preferred not to spend it. So the shippen barn fell down, hay was mouldy, grass became thin, mud became thick and the thorn hedges became raggedy. Why waste money when sticks and oaths made the animals do one's bidding? Such is the way with cruelty.

But at Hawkridge there was kindness too, and it came in the form of something that could easily be mistaken for a hedgehog. However, hedgehogs don't wear woven caps of moss at Yule or carry a cup of wonder as did the prickyback, a small bundle of year-round fairy helpfulness. During summer he rubbed ointments of herbs on cows noses and around cows eyes to ease the worry of flies, and in winter his gentle words eased the chill. All the prickyback asked for in return was fresh creamy milk. Milk to make the cheesi-crumb, the everyday food of bogle folk.

If the Green Man's daughter had a favourite among the creatures that creep and fly it was probably the prickyback. Every Yule she would give Scruff-bundle a cap of woven moss to wear upon his head to make him, she thought, very fancy dressed. Sadly every Yule the prickyback would lose the cap among the thorns of one of Fustilugs hedges.

"Splish-splosh-sploodle, splishy-sploshy-sploodle", sang the prickyback happily as he udder-tugged into his cup of wonder that was never full and never empty. A present from the Green Man's daughter.

To the bogles that lived in and under the trees with souls the prickyback was called Scruffbundle. For as they said: "What you see is what you get". What the bogles got with Scruffbundle was a waddling dishevelment. He looked as though he had just stepped out of a hedge. Of course to the miserable skele-tal cows that splodged mud in Fustilugs's fields this was just what Scruff-bundle always did do.

As every true hedgehog made a winter curl of leaf-ball sleep, Scruffbundle continued his milking but from udders saggy and dry the milk was thin, not creamy at all. Soon the cup of wonder was almost dry too, for that is the way with cruelty. And bogle tummies rumbled with cheesicrumb longing. Some-thing had to be done.

A prickyback could do magic when faced by badness, magic that by the making of promises could be undone. He and the Green Man's daughter hatched a plan.

On a night of frost-white trees the Green Man's daughter span her wind music. A sound that made the foxes cry and badgers bark, owls shriek and stags roar. A cacophony of night-noise bringing Fustilugs and Flotch befud-dled beneath the moon. A night-noise leading them to where the thorn hedges were raggedy and where, moon-beam shy, stood the prickyback with his cup of wonder almost quite empty. He pointed humbly at Fustilugs cows.

"Thief! Nasty prickyback urchin!" dribbled Fustilugs.

"Teat tugger!" sniggered Flotch nastily.

The Green Man's daughter ceased her spinning. The night-noise stopped. The only sounds were the sad lowing of cows and the rasping breaths of the drunken pair.

"Sinwiggles-sinwaggles-sinworms slide," whispered Scruffbundle softly. And just like that Fustilugs and Flotch slid, transformed into a pair of fat, slithering, slowworms for one whole night and one whole day. "Long-cripples, long-cripples, long-cripples mates", sang the prickyback gleefully.

The bogles watched with relief. Their rumbling tummies were over. From that day forward the cup of wonder became fuller and fuller. Behind the windows that bled candlelight, corks stopped in bottles. And folk thought that the mouth of Fustilugs Blowmaunger must have felt better without that cow-tongue.

Never again did Fustilugs ask for a favour with a promise to pay later. Instead he began to pay what he owed. And the farm animals all agreed that he kept his cross-patch promises. Flotch became hard-warking and strong. Fresh straw filled the rebuilt shippen barn. Hedges were tended so Scruffbundle could wear the same woven moss cap for many years and keep a collection of others.

Flotch even made Fustilugs a water-pump so that at Hawkridge there would be running water on the top. Unfortunately Flotch could never make it work. Both bogle and prickyback agreed forgiveness shouldn't come easy.

Oh yes, at Hawkridge the sinworms writhed; and there remains a rumour among some country dwellers that hedgehogs drink milk from the udders of cows.

TWELVE

Snow Cats and Chilly Dogs

"A lot of people like snow. I find it to be an unnecessary freezing of water."
Carl Reiner, American film director, writer and comedian.

We had caught the turmoil from El Niño, the warming of the tropical seas of the Pacific, despite being thousands of miles away. Warm air from El Niño had shot up into the stratosphere and shunted a surge of cold air from the Arctic down across Exmoor.

My dear wife in true Captain Oates fashion had already set off for Minehead and work. I admired her. Outside the warped blue front door it was rather inclement. I opened the warped blue front door a smidgen and the cat looked at me, her upright still in pyjama bottoms, and appeared to say, "Seriously?". Then, encouraged by a gentle boot up the bum, her legs pretty much disappeared into cold white stuff. The small brown mouse with a limp living behind the patio tub was endangered again.

I went online to check the prospects of the local weather and discovered an article of grit and determination:

"With snow forecast for Exmoor today, people are being urged to make sure roadside grit is left on site for everyone to share. Cllr Steven Pugsley, chairman of the Exmoor Panel, which unites many parishes across the moor, said: 'Grit is placed at known trouble spots and people are welcome to use the grit to make these areas safer. However, the grit is not intended for use on private property. If the weather worsens again, people who take the grit for their own use could be putting others in their community at risk. We are asking that people put their community first and make sure that there's enough to go around at these trouble spots, particularly when conditions are bad and it is hard for vehicles to get through to replenish the supplies.'"

Way to go, Bright Ember, I thought, my publisher's published. Then the phone rang. It was my wife on her mobile. "You're in which hedge?" I said … "The nasty corner at Rooks Nest? … Oh, the very nasty one in Elworthy … There's no sign of any grit? … Have you got a shovel? … Yes? Good" … Have you got food and drink? … You want me to come and rescue you?!"

Only occasionally do I think owning a mobile phone is a useful thing. This was one such time. The problem is, and call me old-fashioned, I don't own one. Needless to say twenty minutes later at Elworthy Cross I had had to abandon my own car that had slithered and slipped, and go wife searching on foot into a blizzard of the biggest snow flakes I've ever seen falling from a sky of lead. All around me was chaos with the exception of the smug that drove four-wheel-drives. A wheel-spinning orange Sainsbury's home delivery van was going every which way but the intended direction of forwards. A largish lorry arriving down hill did a dramatic full three-sixty degree skid at the junction, its rictus-grinning driver gripping the steering wheel maniacally. A tearful taxi-driver shouted into his mobile that no way could he get to Withypool however inconvenient it might be for 'the fare'. Other vehicles formed an unmoving jam. Those that tried to move shunted one another. I had cold feet.

There was no sign of my wife. I stomped well passed Elworthy's very nasty corner. Through the falling flakes a van came towards me. I waved it down and it stopped sideways. "Have you seen a little red car anywhere?" I asked.

"A Fiat 500? Yup, I passed it headed very slowly towards Monksilver a few minutes ago. The lady driver looked very worried. Now help give me a push will you."

As the van's engine noise faded the only sound I heard was of complaining sheep making a racket as they moved across a nearby field. Eerie stuff. But things could have been worse. Just to cheer me up as I gingerly headed back to my car, thankfully pointing downhill towards sanctuary, I recalled the last great 'Ammil', a Dartmoor term referring to a coating of ice, that delayed my youthful return to university for the start of the spring term back in '82.

The snow dump that arrived that long ago January coating the branches of Exmoor trees thawed then froze again in extreme cold. Each and every twig was left encased in ice, twinkling in the light, turning pale pink and gold at sunrise and sunset. It was wonderous. Along the coastline the sea froze in Exmoor's harbours. The down side was the weight of ice collapsing numerous power cables that led to cold comfort salads and candles. My shiver of recollection were conjoined with Elworthy shivers as I started the car engine.

It was a while later, and thankful to be safe again behind the warped blue front door, that I rang my wife's workplace. She still hadn't arrived. I rang her mobile. No reply. After pacing around the house, I tried ringing again. Success. "You switched your phone off to save its battery in case I called? … I'm glad you're safe … Two men pushed you out of the hedge? Wonderful … You felt much better knowing I was coming to rescue you? I'm very glad … Where are you now? … Monksilver? … What are doing there? … Ah, waiting for Summer … Absolutely. Love you, too."

In our age of global warming I went outside to cool down and caught sight of old Len pouring sea salt on his garden path. I went along for a gossip to get the morning's adventure off my chest. Was it '50 or '51, he tried to recall, when the Vicar of Withypool turned up to take Sunday Service on a tractor. He could remember 'the big uns' of '47, a time of wartime rationing lacking both labour and snowploughs and '63.

Singing with the Exton Village Minstrels, and as he drives his tractor Tony Takle, greying now but with eyebrows as black as Labour Chancellor Alastair Darling, lived at Kendle Farm ever since he bought the place at auction when he was twenty-five with borrowed money as old farmers shook their head. His memories of '47 were mixed up with others of his childhood like two elephants plodding through Wheddon Cross and his mum giving them six buckets of water to drink. They most likely dunked their trunks with a 'Danke'. The pachyderms were part of Edward Fossett and Sons, an Irish circus, which before the war was known as Heckenberg's Berlin Tower Circus, and was on route between Minehead and Dulverton.

Tony could recall the school bus being unable to get from Minehead to Wheddon Cross for eleven weeks although this wasn't the fault of the elephants but due to snow. With it drifting as high as the telephone posts David and his school friends had 'a whale of a time'. One of them, David Clarbull, fell down a snow crevice on the way to Dunkery and was lucky to get out alive.

As a sheep farmer Tony won cups at Taunton and Cutcombe shows for his sheepy mongrels that were a mixture of grey faced Suffolk, Closewools, Exmoor Horns and those Dutch sheep with the wow factor, Texels. He did once keep pigs until one of his his sows got out of her pen and become a lamb killer. On seeing the sow with a lamb dangling from her chops Tony knew he and she must part company. In the end he went the whole hog and sentenced all his porkies to be sold at Taunton market.

But as winters go, the debate still rages in Tony's head whether '63 was worse because so much salt was used that it had to be imported from Spain.

Certainly, Len plumps for '63. "That salt was fer Exmoor as a whole, not just me path," Len chuckled, before describing how he dug a tunnel from front door to daylight when his entire cottage was covered. The pig-like grunts and 'pruks' of ravens and the caw of rooks were the only inhuman sounds he remembers hearing other than the 'ba-ba-ba' of helicopters. Farms received drops of much needed supplies. Notoriously, Warren Farm at Simonsbath became accessible only by pony or on foot for a period of seventy-four days before a tractor managed it. To Len's mind, the conditions of '63 were probably worse than in '47 but as he said, "when yous a little 'un even the snowmen seem bigger."

Before the age of the snowplough, being out in Exmoor snow was more than just an adventure, it was mortifying. An inquest in December 1320 into the death of a Porlock girl was the first written record of heavy snow on Exmoor. The unfortunate lass was buried in snow whilst trying to walk home from North Molton. There must obviously have been snow deaths before the fourteenth century and certainly there have been many sad stories since. Most were from the time before the coming of the beech hedge when buried places became hard to recognise. But you can't win. The beech hedge has become the mortuary of shelter seeking sheep as well as creating other concerns.

Contemporary lowlanders like Len and I had it easy. My friend Mark, on the other hand, a struggling filmmaker and a musician in his mid thirties who's played Glastonbury chose to be a Dunkery dweller. "We creatives can be anywhere. All we need is a plug socket and broadband connection," he said, almost by means of an excuse. Well, full praise to Exmoor keeping up with trends but on more than one occasion I've thought Mark's 'anywhere' was a bit extreme. He and his partner Fiona together with their black quick-learning lurcher pup, Belle, were snowbound in a remote farm cottage down a secret narrow lane going nowhere other than to isolation. And the log pile was dwindling.

In old Exmoor fashion, the cottage, although built of stone, was clad on the outside with corrugated iron sheeting decorated in peeling buttermilk paint. Inside there was scant heating to allay the damp. A rusted decades-old iron hook screwed into a kitchen ceiling beam was substantial enough to have hung a haunch of venison from, a temptation, that to his credit, Mark had resisted. Now deer kept to the skeletal woods as, not far away, the coats of wild ponies became frost encrusted.

A snowplough did make it down the lane to Hawkington, but it proved to be more trouble than it was worth by coming without grit. The fluffy snow compacted by the vehicle's tyres froze to become an ice sheet upon which more snow dollops fell. Mark thought the driver just wanted to 'get in and get out as fast as possible' as the ploughs themselves were not immune to dangers.

In a still talked about story from 1978, when lanes were blocked for ten weeks, a snowplough became snow buried and the bunch of men going to rescue the driver were buried in an avalanche. It was the hedgebanks that were the problem. Because of them snow collects in lanes the length and breadth of Exmoor and there is nowhere for snowploughs to push it. And with the hedges shading the lanes the snow often stays put despite melting in the fields on either side.

As the car took on the shape of an igloo and metre high drifts lay in the hedge-banked lane Mark and Fiona had predicaments of real concern – heat, food, horse and Sir Ranulph Fiennes's mother.

Drummer, Fiona's barrel of a skewbald Irish cob with feathered coronets, who would attempt jumping a fence only if he knew there was something to munch on the other side, was stabled at Luckwell Bridge. And as is the way of horses he needed hay, mucking out and TLC. Administering such creature comforts meant a twice daily two mile struggle for Fiona across snow deep fields. She got the short straw because, although only little, she was a hardy Scot from Fife. Naming her plodder Drummer was the obvious choice. His creaky motorised horsebox was the life-saver that allowed Fiona to bundle along the gritted main road to Wootton Courtenay for her work as the carer of the famous explorer's mum.

The lesser priorities of food and heat were Mark's responsibility. Hunter gathering from the only shop in Wheddon Cross was a determined morning's yomp. The pretty view of white hill and combe over the garden hedge was indeed one to die for should one feel disinclined.

Regarding the heating problem, Harold, the rugged but no longer youthful cattle and sheep farmer who was Mark and Fiona's landlord, stopped by on his tractor with a helpful question for Mark: "Ave yer got a chainsaw, boy?"

Mark waited for more words of advice to flow forth from Harold, like where to go for a suitable tree and how to get sawn logs back to the rapidly chilling cottage. But Harold stayed silent on such practicalities. He just adjusted his flat cap, and muttered, "Yep, be good if yer got a chainsaw." And drove off leaving Mark to ponder how old you have to be on Exmoor until you cease to be called, 'boy'.

What to do? With an upstairs window slightly ajar, Mark will stick out the barrel of his air rifle and wait, letting his beard grow, dragging on slow burning roll-ups, his cold hands comforted by fingerless woollen gloves. Any desultory rabbit, pheasant or pigeon coming into range meets with a hopeful pot shot for the hot pot. Success is rewarded by bouncing and barks when Belle's called on to 'go fetch'. A kill, she knows, is shared three ways.

Happily, I knew Mark was still in the land of the living when I received a lyrical email:

"'When the sun burst forth at last upon a world of white, what he brought was neither warmth, nor cheer, nor hope of softening; only a clearer shaft of cold from the violet depths of sky.' R.D. Blackmore, *Lorna Doone*, Chapter 42."

Mark was quoting the man who once described a snow blanketed Exmoor as being "softened as if the hand of a woman had been upon it". I emailed back with my concerns about snow fever affecting some generic groups when snow's been sat on the ground for ten days or more.

However, there were others just as deserving of sympathy who had also been cut off for a similar amount of time. At Exmoor Zoo at South Stowford visitors and deliveries had ceased. The few humans living on site were press-ganged into looking after the animals' welfare. Only two keepers, having to stomp three and a half miles of local lanes that suffered from drifted snow and compacted ice, got to work. It was a skeleton staff for bivvering residents that deeply regretted their place of captivity.

Although, given the zoo's five hundred and seventy five animals there were notable exceptions among the two hundred or so different species of animals and birds. Firstly, there was Freddie, a stowaway red African toad. He was the zoo's latest arrival, after hopping out of the sun into a shady rucksack he had discovered on the banks of the Zambezi. Subsequently, after the toss and turn of two air flights he astonishingly reached Britain. His discovery under a trainer earned a degree of fame with an appearance on CBBC *Newsround* as he showed off his bijou, centrally heated, new Exmoor home complete with private pool.

Then there were the reindeer. Derek Gibson, the zoo's head-keeper reminded the outside world that, "not every animal dislikes the snow - the reindeer with their big feet and thick fur coats are in their element enjoying every moment." Well, bully for them. Certainly, the cheetahs in their frosty enclosure wouldn't have empathised. For what it was worth the education officer also managed the struggle to work. Perhaps it was his job to teach the eclectic mix of fauna that getting fed warmed porridge, jacket potatoes and cooked vegetables would be good for them and keep them warm. Such cuisine might have seemed a tad too exotic for the wary a long way from home.

As snowploughs cleared the main road some deliveries managed to get reasonably close. It left the zoo's quad bike to be put to good use, dragging the zoo van up the minor road to the A399 and transporting feed and materials with difficulty back to the zoo. The thaw would be welcomed by feather, paw and claw.

My wife and I welcomed it, too.

Reindeer apart I don't think any Exmoor resident either four-legged, winged or upright would concur with a couple of lines on the 'Visit Exmoor and West Somerset' webpage. "Winter," it claims, "is a magical time."

THIRTEEN

Wheezing Whistles and Hippy Goats

"When I was a kid, I went to the store and asked the guy, 'Do you have any toy train schedules?'"
Stephen Wright, American actor and writer.

As he stretched to the top shelf of the tallest cupboard I remember my Dad's traumatising words, "Don't ever touch." Ever since Dad first wowed a very small me with his Hornby train set with its miniature steam locomotives of exquisite detail kept ever so carefully and handled like sacred relics, almost too precious to see the light of day in their original cardboard boxes, I knew such toys for boys were ones to be appreciated from a distance. But I felt deprived.

And working artistically on crude animations in their Canterbury cowshed Oliver Postgate and Peter Firmin did me no favours. Through a poor signal snowstorm of black and white television images my childhood head was filled by the delights of *Ivor the Engine* going 'Fissh-te-cum-fissh-te-cum'; dragons lived in his firebox and his driver Jones The Steam kept a fox in Mrs Portly's hatbox. As Ivor's world turned to colour I learned that he was green ticked off nicely with red buffer plates and that with the help of paper, sticks, coal and water Jones the Steam could make a cup of tea from Ivor's boiler. Little engines became practical things that I yearned to get my naughty little hands on.

So you can only imagine my delight when recently near Martinhoe again I took my eyes off the main road for a split second as I passed Woody Bay station and took a deep intake of incredulous breath before exclaiming, "Oh my word, twin Ivors!" Excited, I took the next turn into what was left of the Lynton & Barnstaple Railway. And I discovered a phoenix yawning after more than seventy years of sleeping in what had become the narrow gauge world of the unpaid volunteer.

Furtive anoraks cuddling cameras and camcorders wandered around the platform where a thin grey haired lady, seemingly immune to the chill wind, dressed two tone in white shirt, tie and black slacks, held a station guard's flag. I named her Miss White. Judging by the colour of the oil smeared, tummy tight, overalls, the little green engines were being nursed by Mister Orange, Mister Purple and Mister Blue. Although Mister O and Mister P ignored me, Mister B, I soon fathomed, was called Wederall, a chap who had been playing with trains all his life, and who kept sandwiches and a flask of tea amongst the rags and clutter of his toolbox. Oh, how I envied him his contentment.

After adjusting the obligatory flat cap and removing a heavy-duty firebox glove so as to stroke, with calloused fingers, his neatly trimmed white whisker beard, Wederall introduced me to the two locomotives I'd seen from the road. Axe and Sid, both christened after Devon rivers, had their names proudly emblazoned on plates welded to their respective bodywork that shone, to my mind, with equal brilliance, proof of loving hours of polishing. My close inspection showed, however, that they weren't twins at all.

Axe, the more 'Ivorish' of the two was feeling fine and full of steam despite his age. Built by Kerr, Stuart & Co Ltd at Stoke-on-Trent in 1915 Axe and was one of the seventy 'Joffre' Class engines that the French government ordered for service on the Western Front.

Sid was a German built Maffei. Of similar age to Axe, he was suffering from some leaky tubes and was a bit poorly. As if to prove the point, from beneath the pines and beeches near the station platform and some red carriages Sid gave an asthmatic wheeze of a whistle and let go pitiful steam clouds from several orifices that were only capable of enshrouding a small tree of heaven. His funnel puffed out 'fumata bianca' then 'fumata nera' as if he was still undecided on the Pope. Wederall thought it rather alarming.

Sid was indeed in need of some TLC, but money, I understood, was in short supply following the mile long line extension out from Woody Bay being completed in 2006. As a result, Killington Lane, once a field stop on route to Parracombe Halt, had become the current terminus. A 'temporary' arrangement perhaps, but at least it offered a regular 'point-to-point' for man-made horsepower and a sensation that broke the boredom of sheep. However, Killington wasn't that much less lacking in facilities than Parracombe Halt had ever been. From my memory I dredged up an image of the Halt that I'd seen in an old sepia photo taken in 1923. A desultory young fellow in shorts and long socks stood between the tracks. There was an open gate through which he must have dashed, too late for the already departed. On the platform was a 'waiting room' comprised of a sloped roofed, windowless wooden shed with an arched entrance open to the elements.

Being almost 'one-in-fifty', the journeys to and from Woody Bay are about as steep as that 'waiting room' roof had been. And it's all uphill from Killington despite the gobbledegook of railway parlance that says one is travelling down. For this one must blame tradition. London was always up, whereas anything away from the Great Metropolis was down.

However, with one mile of the Lynton and Barnstaple line restored there were still eighteen to go to rebuild the whole of the railway's original length. Closed by the Southern Railway long before the birth of the preservation movement, the L&B has achieved cult status with the world's railway enthusiasts, helped, no doubt, by one of its locos becoming legendary. The engine was exported to Brazil before the outbreak of the Second World War and was never seen or heard of again.

It was a bit like Woody Bay itself, whose station was built in part to serve the expected development of a local resort nearby funded by a Colonel Benjamin Lake, an entrepreneurial Orpington solicitor. He expected doing great holiday trade from passing coastal steamers and he had a pier built in the bay. In 1898, the Lynton & Barnstaple Railway arrived with its unfulfilled plans for a branch line to run down towards the shore. Had it done so it might have given Lynton's environmentally friendly funicular Cliff Railway a run for the money in grockle wallets. That had been opened eight years earlier by Lady of the Manor, Mrs Jeune, saving knackered ponies and donkeys hired at 6d a time the woes of many a burden up steep Lynmouth Hill.

Sod's Law intervened for the Colonel, however. His pier was destroyed by a storm that brought heavy seas before any trade could be established. And the resort's development was abandoned in 1900 when the unfortunate Colonel went bankrupt. For his pains he was sentenced to twelve years in prison, for using clients' savings to fund his Woody Bay chimera.

From an inside pocket, Wederall, with a heavy sigh, produced a photo of Axe taken the previous autumn. The little engine looked resplendent carrying a garland of golden chrysanthemums. It was an annual thing commemorating the wreath bearing the words "Perchance it is not dead, but sleepeth" laid on the stop-block at Barnstaple Town station in September 1935. The gesture became the inspiration for local railways buffs to undertake the line's restoration. Certainly, this was Wederall's own pipe dream and there had been executive talk to fuel it.

I suggested that instead of using chrysanths the commemorative wreath should be made of Himalayan knotweed. The noxious, spear-like leaved, hollow-stemmed, invasive pest now subject to the Exmoor Knotweed Control Project is reputed to have taken hold when a twit of a clergyman sprinkled seeds along the path of the L&B line. Forming dense stands of tall canes during the summer and with roots going down twelve metres getting rid of it isn't the easiest of tasks. Jungle beckons.

It's unsurprising the L&B has been termed the 'last railway adventure'. However, the plan does exist to provide a massive boost to the Lyn Valley by taking the railway to Lynton one day. Tourists would then chuff through a landscape of stone walls, horses and farm beasts, with the sea shining in the distance. But just restoring the line from Woody Bay to Killington was estimated to have cost well in excess of a million pounds and Wederall appeared downbeat about future progress. There were neither the funds nor the planning consent to go any further. The one glimmer of optimism came by showing the current micro-demonstration was operating successfully so that QED a full rebuilding was potentially feasible. Although on the question of profitability, Wederall remained a little quiet. I'm sure the spirit of Colonel Lake feels for him.

At the time of my visit Wederall was mourning the loss of Holwell Castle. It had been moved, he said.

"What? Like the location of the Battle of Bosworth?" I asked. A field as featureless as any in England at Alf Oliver's arable farm, just off the old Roman road from Atherstone to Leicester had just been revealed as the true site two miles adrift from where it used to be. But surely Holwell, with its deep ditch surrounding a circular motte and kidney-shaped bailey, had always been where the Norman Martin de Tours, the first lord of Parracombe, put it. Why he did so was debatable. Perhaps to protect and supervise silver mining in the area around Combe Martin and intimidate folk for the collection taxes at the River Heddon bridging point. Or then again it could just of been a hunting lodge protecting the Royal Forest. Who's to say?

Voicing these thoughts to Wederall made him look bemused.

"Don't know what you're on about," he said, "The Holwell Castle was a lovely diesel that left the L&B a short while ago for the Golden Valley Railway in Derbyshire. It was sad to see her go."

"Been forced into a cull?" I unwisely queried in jest.

And indeed Wederall wasn't amused. "Our engines have got off lightly compared to the goats," he said.

"Goats? Which goats?"

"The feral beggers in the Valley of the Rocks. They say all but fifty are going to be shot. Lynton and Lynmouth Town Council have given the orders. No kidding. Can't say I approve."

Nor did I. For years I had taken events in the Valley of the Rocks far too lightly. Heck, wild goats had lived there for at least a millennium in different guises and were hinted at in the Domesday Book.

The modern goats weren't killers like the wild goats T. H. Cooper recorded in his 1853 guidebook that butted sheep over the cliffs when the reputed witch Aggie Norman, undoubtedly the model for the witch Mother Meldrum in *Lorna Doone*, lived seasonally in the valley; nor were they related to the goats of the cashmere variety that roamed the valley during the first half of the twentieth century that sprang from Queen Victoria's royal herd in Windsor Great Park.

I remember the powers-that-be sacking the fine-bearded, short-coated, white common or garden Saenan goats in '76 as punishment for their misdemeanours. The whole herd had liked to amble into the town to bin rummage, chomp fresh flowers in window boxes or those left lying about the cemetery. Yet, wanting to keep a capra style tourist attraction, what to do?

The municipal idea had been to replace the flora guzzlers with impeccably behaved, hirsute, hippy looking rare breed Cheviots from Northumberland. Unfortunately, the idea backfired as three Saenan billies, for some reason or other, found themselves left behind when the hippies arrived. And with Nature being as it is, the breeds crossbred very successfully, rock leap on Ragged Jack, leer from ledges on Castle Rock, peer from crags on the Cheesewring, scree slope slither, eye-ball folk through gorse bush and bracken fern or simply snooze in the car park.

Then, three years ago in spring 2007, I picked up an email sent by an old acquaintance inviting me to a liquid lunch at Lynton's dog friendly Beggars *Roost*. The acquaintance in question was a lady, with a farty Bassett hound in tow, who preferred to remain anonymous other than me saying she had strong links with the Lynton Feral Goat Preservation Society.

The story she had to tell was like something out of *Midsomer Murders* although now the victims weren't human. Near the Poet's Corner shelter in the Valley of the Rocks, a lady friend of hers came across a pile of green peppers that had been hollowed out and filled with the white crystals and blue seeds. Suspicious, the friend bagged the veg and took it home to show her pharmacist husband. He identified caustic soda. Around the same time frame, shots had been heard echoing around the valley in the early hours of the morning. Someone unknown was out shooting. Whether it was out of malice, or for trophies or meat, noone could say. The only certainty was that the goats were being targeted. My acquaintance hoped a liquid lunch might encourage me to raise awareness by doing a news feature.

Poisons and bullets all sounded a bit too heavy for my liking. Sorry, I said in apology, but I had to be somewhere else. Attending a film festival in far away Eastern Europe suddenly felt like a damn fine idea. As fate would have it I bumped into the lady a few months later as I trolled up on a whim, hopeful of horny chaos, to film a roundup.

She told me she'd had another great idea. Why not bolster the Valley of the Rocks mongrels with new blood from Morocco's Atlas Mountains? There, goats had wondrous tree climbing abilities in their forage for Argan oil nuts. So just by spraying local sycamore fruits with Argan oil one created a major new tourist attraction and help tackle the problem of the invidious Sycamore.

"I have sympathy for sycamores," I said. "Sometimes they can be quite dense.'"

I also had sympathy for the goaty crowd gathered under a large tarpaulin that offered shade near two horseboxes. One was used by Rachel the vet as an examination room, the other acting as a death chamber for the infirm.

Catchers brought the goats into Rachel's box and onwards to other handlings that may have ensued. Out of kindness mums and their kids were kept together. The smaller goats were carried, the mediums were pulled through by their horns but the gurt billies needed to be persuasively yanked by two musclemen. Every goats personal details were noted. Teeth and gums provided clues of age, ears hid parasites; and the whites of eyes tipped off anaemia. As background observers, a couple of policemen kept fidgeting with boredom.

Three years on and back on Woody Bay station platform, as I watched a stoat pop in and out of a neat stack of railway sleepers on the far side of the tracks, Wederall claimed the Council wanted to shoot a hundred and twenty healthy animals.

"Stoats?" I said.

"Haven't you bin listenin'? Goats," said Wederall.

It was my turn to call the anonymous lady and flick through my precious black moleskin book of numbers. This was now indeed a news story, I thought, only to be told, after finally getting a call back from several left messages that it wasn't.

"Sorry, you've missed the boat," she said. "The Lynton Feral Goat Preservation Society has already safeguarded the goats' future. They're all going to Surrey. The Surrey Wildlife Trust and the Ministry of Defence have signed a conservation grazing agreement and the goats are eagerly awaited."

"Ministry of Defence? What? Are they going to use the goats as mine detectors?" She cut me off.

By the end of the day my wife observed I was being a little gruff. Perhaps I needed to let off some steam, she suggested.

FOURTEEN

Those Persons from Porlock

"I am a big believer in early intervention."
Temple Grandin, American author and inventor of the hug machine.

Although it had been a pity to miss the Porlock Weir Beer Festival, there had been something I wanted to do and I had put half a day in March aside to do it. The other half I intended to use fishing. Saturday selling out of the back of his white van in a Wivey car park, the fish man's parting of knowledge that there were shoals of cod in the Western Approaches and always had been, never translated to Porlock Bay. But hope sprang eternal.

A week earlier, a pensioner couple had waved me to a stop in Simonsbath in front of the substantial white house James Boevey a Dutch-born London banker-cum-solicitor built and where according to *Aubrey's Brief Lives* he ate a lot of chicken, kept a candle and notebook by his bed, and owned many books on magic and witchcraft including a still surviving handwritten list by Elias Ashmole, the celebrated astrologer and alchemist.

James purchased Exmoor Forest from the Crown in 1652 and going by the date '1654' carved into an oak beam above the old kitchen fireplace this was when James commenced building his isolated house far from the ravages of the Great Plague and Great Fire that would affect London a decade later. And James's pad remained the only house within the Forest boundaries until the nineteenth century when John Knight, a Midlands ironmaster, bought three quarters of the Royal forest for fifty grand or £5 an acre with big plans. But in truth he and his son Frederic lost a lot of money.

The waving pensioners appeared as though they had lost something, too. They asked whether I knew about an air crash that might have happened close by, maybe at Cheriton. It was one of those weird internet stories often found by accidental click. Wanting something to do to break their daily routine, they had decided to follow the story up. All I could do was shrug. In return I got the key words 'Scob Hill' and 'bomber' off them.

My own Google search found an anecdote from the summer of 1989 posted by a Roz Gray:

"At the top of Scob Hill what appeared to be a B17 bomber appeared in the sky - there was no sound and suddenly it dived and appeared to crash among the hillsides beyond. We were so convinced we had witnessed a real crash despite the silence and lack of smoke we drove at speed towards Cheriton and on nearly into Simonsbath trying to find a crash site.

"We knew what the plane was immediately when we saw it, as my father was a WW2 R.A.F. navigational officer and both my ex husband and I had worked within an aviation cultural archive. I could sight and name military planes from childhood. There were crashes in that part of the world during the war - I know of one I recall hearing about at Porlock Weir . We didn't see anything of the usual identifiers, the planes markings, numbers or even the artwork which was common in U.S.A.A.F. planes. In the sky the object appeared to be dark grey with not even a glint of metal in the sunlight and it was only afterwards that we realised no plane flying low in sun looks like that."

I immediately wanted to learn more about the Porlock Weir crash. I knew there had been a memorial stone in memory of a wartime loss placed nearer to Porlock itself than the Weir, which at the time exported pit props cut in local forests to South Wales. This was only fair, as during the eighteenth and nineteenth centuries coal had come the other way and an early dream of sending Exmoor bounty to Wales came to nowt. The plan hatched by Frederic Knight to build a mineral railway to carry copper and iron ore from the family's Wheal Eliza mine at Simonsbath to Porlock Weir had to be abandoned. What Exmoor offered up was Scrooge-like and wasn't worth the effort.

As for the memorial, this had been erected at the back of the shingle ridge.

This was nothing to do with the St Dubricius church that had shingles, that's to say, cleaved oak shingles on the odd, truncated spire. No, I mean the ridge just west of the rough pebble causeway. That memorial stone, I thought, must be what Roz was on about and it was where I aimed for first thing on that put aside day.

Robert Southey, before becoming poet laureate, wrote an insipid sonnet as he bibbled at Porlock's Ship Inn bar in 1798. He managed to get it published in the *Morning Post*. Lines included: 'Porlock, thy verdant vale so fair to sight,' and 'the channel grey, Circling its surges in thy level bay'. Nowadays, despite some calling Porlock 'Lala Land', ever since the yellow coloured Teletubby stayed in the village, I reserved a soft spot for the place upon hearing there were strippers opposite the Castle Hotel. But before anyone gets their knickers in a twist, let me quickly add that they worked in the village tannery. And having lived in the old Bampton tannery for many years, I felt empathic. Among the rough lot of thirty or so guddlers employed at Porlock's was Jimmy Steele. And he, to use the Exmoor phrase, was 'not quite exactly'. Only late in life did Jimmy summon up the courage to travel by train. Taking himself off to Minehead station he bewildered the booking clerk by demanding "an outside ticket, please. You don't catch me a-gooin' inside them affairs."

In his day, Jimmy had been a legend, as was also Sidney Tucker, huntsman to the 'D&S' during the first couple of decades of the twentieth century. Locally notorious for filling his Porlock cottage full of stags' heads and all sorts of trophies and mementoes, Sidney also kept a collection of hunting knives. On the word of his widow, Sidney killed more than two thousand stags. The old hunter was a walking genocide.

It's saying the obvious that Porlock has changed a bit over the years. Names like Jimmy Steele and Sidney Tucker have given way to those more contemporary.

This I learnt after I came across a pair of well wrapped up, stubbly, twenty-somethings, half-heartedly scatting small pebbles at a target of an empty lager can sat on a boulder of the sort common thereabouts. With the wind whipping spume and spray off Porlock Bay I've always found the stretch of pebbles and submarine fossilised forest between Gore Point and Bossington somewhat desultory. The men's aimless occupation didn't help.

They must have spotted me scratching my head; the stone I was looking for had gone. I had ambled down the farm track leading off Sparkhayes Lane and across fields, full of confidence. Now salt-licked air, successfully biting through my chin-warming scarf as I searched, dented it further. "Mislaid summat, mate?" came the shout.

Warily, I explained, they having introduced themselves as Sneeze and Stew da Spliff.

"Sorry mate, it moved, 'bout three years ago," said Sneeze, whose eyes and nose pointed to him being allergic to something, possibly Stew's herbal roll-up. Feeling public-spirited I told a short moving anecdote about my acquaintance 'Hippy Nick'. He had given up spliffs having realised they seriously affected his powers of deliberation. After removing the blue tarpaulin that had for a long while covered the mossed, leaky, thatched roof of his little cob built cottage the dwelling collapsed to rubble leaving Nick the problem of rehoming himself.

Sneeze said that he wanted to move, too. I asked him the silly question: Why?

The village, he whinged, was in the middle of nowhere and all the roads out were steep, forty-five degrees in places. There was no music, no films, no female talent, no decent beach, just pebbles the size of footballs, and plenty of 'bloody trees'. When it rained it poured. There were no decent fish and chips. The special Porlock oak jugs that my Nan used to buy you can't get anymore. The people who drove incredibly slowly up Porlock Hill were all in the lawn bowling club, and none of them seemed to like him or his mates much.

I asked Sneeze if he would rather be in Minehead and got a look that Jimmy Steele might have recognised. "Nah," he laughed, "Minehead's just the small village outside Butlins. Anyway, same as Porlock it's downstream from the smelly Avonmouth area. And with Hinkley Point, no wonder we've got the warmest sea in the British Isles."

"Don't knock it," I said. "The piddocks love the peaty, grey clay, beach. So much so, that every Porlock piddock digs itself a burrow and stays cosy in it for the whole of its eight year life. The only thing it exposes is its siphon to filter food from water." My class of two plus a lager can then got a brief lesson about piddocks being toothy, clamlike bivalve molluscs with unique shells. Their clever name's *Pholadidae*. One of the piddock's shells has a set of 'teeth', which it uses to grind away at the Porlock clay to create its tubular burrow.

The piddocks had taken up residence in what was once thick forest where ancient peoples hunted aurochs when the present beach was more than five miles inland. I considered it quite a logical notion that such sea level rise could be put down to the predecessors of the likes of Sneeze and Stew idly lobbing their pebbles into it over bygone ages and concluded, as if proof were needed, both tree trunks and piddocks can be found at low tide as well as the occasional auroch bone.

Sneeze gave a dismissive glance.

The wind seemed to whistle its own incredulity, giving me the cold shoulder, and cause for Stew to chip in: "I like the country air and being away from the city, the feeling that you don't have to make an effort." I nodded my agreement. Did Porlock have any other redeeming factors? I asked.

Sneeze, furrowed his brow in concentrated thought: "The snooker hall where everyone in the area loses their virginity, and you don't need a watch 'cos time here's irrelevant."

Feeling that Sneeze deserved a clock, I left him and Stew to their scatting and headed for the village Visitor Centre where Denise, the manager, was very helpful. Yes, the memorial stone had been moved, lock, stock and barrel. Although she couldn't quite remember why, it was now on the Porlock part of the marsh.

Before retracing my step to find the memorial, I asked her if anything else was new. "Oh yes," she said. "We're offering a free juicing service again this year. The village ladies are very enthusiastic. It's fabulous and we're thrilled to bits." Seeing that I didn't quite know how to take that piece of information, she added dryly: "The old orchard just off the toll road had been given a new lease of life by becoming a community orchard."

It was almost noon by the time I found the simple stone by a wooden footbridge crossing the Hawkcombe Stream. The stone was erected, it was written, by the local British Legion in memory of some unlucky American United States Air Force chaps. They perished when their B24D Liberator bomber crashed on return from a patrol on 29th October 1942. Only one of the eleven crew survived.

Sobered, I went to sea; spending the afternoon going the same way as the tide, fishing with Deaf Derek, a chap of selective hearing. And like the conversation, the fishing wasn't much of a success. Derek, let me explain, was a fishing friend who took me out from time to time from Porlock Weir in his boat that he had named *Lynn Marie Two* after his wife, she being 'number one'.

Sometimes as I stood with rod, tackle and bait box waving arms and shouting from the shore as Derek boat-sat in the middle of harbour engrossed in splicing some or knot tying I felt that I needed a foghorn to attract his attention, a bit similar to the one that used to belong to 'The Guillemot'. If memory serves me right, this also once bobbed here. Ron, the bright-minded owner, a man who self-confessed to having to have a spit and a shit before doing anything, removed the horn and installed it instead into his wife's Morris Traveller. He did so for her own safety making the car sound like a ship in the night when heard approaching down Exmoor lanes. It attacked the senses long before the headlights could be sighted by oncomers. Indeed, the blessed appliance also caused much alarm on many an urban Somerset roundabout.

With problems of communication Derek and I were prone to misunderstanding. While rod-dangling, instead of the usual hobbit shark of a dogfish, I had hooked a splendid specimen of that sea chameleon, the cuttlefish. Conservation minded towards such an advanced mollusc that's related to both squid and octopodes, I threw it back into the waters of Porlock Bay. I thought I was doing the right thing until I caught Derek's eye. There was a welling of tears. 'Oi wanted that for me tank. Oi 'aven't got one of they,' he almost cried. Along with his boat Derek also owned a sea life aquarium just along from the Weir's glass blowers.

And a time before that, I thought Derek had said Porlock herons were pickled in barrels for on-ship eating. I later realised, by raising matters of elocution, it was 'herrings', but not before things had taken their natural course as they always tend to when I pass on useless information to the trusting.

Happily the misunderstanding was sorted out before the publication of a new Exmoor cookbook that also might have included, but didn't, Porlock's traditional dish. Seaweed mush was commonly packed into a crock and sold as 'potted laver' in Bath during the eighteenth century. And still today a few tough stomached Porlock folk beach-comb in pursuit of fresh organic matter. Once collected, edible seaweed is repeatedly washed to remove sand then boiled for hours until it becomes a stiff green mush that can be preserved for about a week. Apparently the salty delight was a favourite dish of poet Sam Coleridge for whom the area was the home of maternal ancestors. It was his fault that the whole person from Porlock malarkey began.

"It's someone from Porlock," said my wife that evening, passing me the phone. She had caught me unawares engrossed in a self debate whether I should play my East Wind or pung with a three bamboo as we played Mah Jong.

Gawd, who could it be? Derek? Must be something to do with hunting for that cuttlefish, again. For God's sake he was as obsessed as Sam's ancient mariner had been over an albatross.

Anyway, thinking I knew whom to expect, I shouted into the phone, 'Derek, hi!' Then after a pregnant pause and considerably quieter, I said, 'Oh, hi Miles.'

"Charles? You alright? Can you can come to a *Local Authors Day*?" said Miles. Porlock's Arts Festival Committee, I gleaned, had been given the go ahead. Miles had been given the job of putting meat on the bones and I was some of its gristle. "We've extended an invitation to Sir Christopher Ondaatje, and Margaret Drabble and her husband Michael Holroyd will possibly be putting their heads around the door."

"Positively a timberyard of authors," I said. "Count me in."

As I put down the phone I cogitated on Margaret getting undeserved stick for her book *The Witch of Exmoor* and also on another famous head that came around the door not far away, at some farmhouse or other near Culbone. Where the great gobbler of seaweed mush was in 1797 when interrupted by the immortal person from Porlock is open to debate. Certainly, one couldn't rely on Sam the opium addict to know his bearings as he composed his poem 'Kubla Khan'.

A lucid Sam was confident that he stayed at a farmhouse "a quarter of a mile from Culbone Church". Out of the possibles, Ash Farm became the best bet, but was about twice the distance. However, this would be to forget the poet mentioned in his dotage that the farm had been called 'Brimstone'. This, some say, may have been a befuddlement of Broomstreet Farm. Yes, admittedly, being two miles from Culbone's St Beuno's church. It's wide of the mark by a fair distance but Sam did know it from other visits. But let's not forget Withycombe Farm that was only about a third of a mile from church and which, I feel, was the most likely place. As fate would have it, the farmhouse itself was demolished in the mid nineteenth century. In Sam's day, though, it had a fine view of a deep natural amphitheatre christened the 'Punch-bowl', through some banter between an army colonel and a naval admiral both of whom had been chasing a hare with harrier hounds.

According to Frederick Snell the conversation went something like this:

Colonel: "I say, supposing that the hollow under us were balked up at the other end, and filled with water, how many men-of-war could ride comfortably there?"

Admiral: "I should think three first-class ships of war might manoeuvre."

Colonel: "Then egad! I've drunk as much port as could float three of His Majesty's seventy-fours."

Whichever roof was over Sam's head the story that surrounds 'Kubla Khan' has been decided upon. Having taken three grains of opium to relieve what Samuel called at different times "a dysentery" or "a slight indisposition" he went into a trance. During it he composed two or three hundred lines of poetry "without any sensation of consciousness of effort". When he awoke he held in his mind 'a distinct recollection of the whole' and started to write it down. It was then that the person from Porlock interrupted him from his writing for about an hour, after which, the goodly poet was dismayed to find that "though he still retained some vague and dim recollection of the general purport of the vision, yet, with the exception of some eight or ten scattered lines and images, all the rest had passed away like the images on the surface of a stream into which a stone has been cast. . . "

I don't want to be a killjoy to Royston Connor, the landlord of the Ship Inn, who suggests the Porlock chap was someone from the pub asking Sam to settle his drinks bill, but there are those out there in the world who think Sam was just telling a big fib. The poet Roger McGough suggested this view in one of his own poems, saying "I think he got stuck."

Yet, by introducing the distraction that destroyed his train of thought, Sam created a phenomenon that entered the psyche of the arts. The "Person from Porlock", "Man from Porlock", or just "Porlock" have become literary allusions to unwanted intruders. For example, in Vladimir Nabokov's *Lolita*, a character checks into a motel under the pseudonym A. Person, Porlock, England. In Arthur Conan Doyle's novel *The Valley of Fear*, Sherlock Holmes is interrupted in his labours by a letter from the pseudonymous Fred Porlock, an informant within Moriarty's organization. Porlock's identity is never revealed.

The Person from Porlock is a science fiction story by Raymond F. Jones published in *Astounding* magazine in 1947, where Coleridge's vision is explained as the remote viewing of a secret colony of aliens living on Earth. One of the aliens deliberately distracts Coleridge before he can write down a full description of the colony.

Then there was the comic book writer Paul Jenkins. During his run on the *Hellblazer* comic series, the character John Constantine, an occult detective, learns that his ancestor, one James Constantine, was 'The Person from Porlock'. What he does not learn, but the reader does, is that James disrupted Sam's opium-sparked dreams so as to prevent a group of angels from feeding Sam what amounted to a propaganda piece for the armies of Heaven.

In 1995, Steve Hawley directed an arty short video film entitled *The Man From Porlock*. Previewed at the National Film Theatre, the film was inspired by Coleridge's poems with an unseen narrator commenting on a stream of images, speculating on the failure of creativity, and the end of language itself. The music for the film was composed and played by the gloriously eccentric Jane Bom-Bane, 'Queen of the Funky Harmonium', and the wearer of mechanical hats. She owns ones that light up and ones with moving parts. Described by the press as 'either a genius or an example of care in the community gone wrong', she gained some national fame with her song, *I've Got A Goldfish Bowl On My Head* that got a slot on Channel 4.

Sam, I'm sure, would have been most impressed and would have thought her a bigger distraction than his ubiquitous Porlock person. "Porlock, I also shall forget thee not", wrote Robert Southey. Indeed, dear sir, indeed.

FIFTEEN

Banishment and Bacteria

"Absence from those we love is self from self - a deadly banishment."
William Shakespeare, English dramatist and poet, 1564-1616.

The cat's tummy had not registered the clock's going forward by an hour so she continued to sofa-doze as the kettle boiled and the world strangely moved about her. On the wetter side of the warped blue front door was a curtain of sleet-cum-rain. The catkin limp corkscrew hazel and the bowed, bedraggled daffodils that shared a waterlogged patio half-barrel seemed disbelieving Exmoor had entered British Summer Time. The olive tree was dead, drowned.

Hopeful of the weather clearing up as the morning went on I left the house to the elements. If I promised to open and close all the gates on route I could cadge a lift in Mark's old battered Land Rover. Not a bad deal, I thought. That way I could get to film what I needed on my Culbone list without having to lug heavy camera kit too far on my tod.

Mark's first foot on the brake was upon Culbone Hill under a patch of blue sky. Amongst a tangle of twisted hobbit pines is a prehistoric stone row that went unnoticed until about thirty years ago. There are at least twenty grey-brown stones, the tallest ones only being knee high. I wanted to record them on a television quality video camera before a new season of fern and bramble growth performed the practiced act of concealment. In the past I had always left it too late in the year and had to content myself with filming viviparous lizards. Some I'd find sunning themselves on stiles or woodland paths. Others would be sulking and licking their wounds.

Often called evets or common lizards because they are, they sun bask not to get a tan the way grockles struggle to do on Minehead beach, but to reach their optimum body temperature, a toasty thirty degrees Celsius. And although I'm not hinting at depravity, their attempts at sex can be violent. Either in late April or during May blokes take their chosen lass in their jaws, and if she's not interested she will give the bloke a very fierce bite. But no evet showed itself that day as I scrabbled around trying to find an angle for an evocative shot.

After Mark had puffed his way through several roll-ups I was ready to move on to the next list item, the Culbone Stone inscribed with a wheeled cross whose stem points to four o'clock, the way to Culbone's St Beuno's church. Beuno was a Welsh holy man and Culbone is simply derived from the old English name for the church, 'Kil Beun'. And at thirty-four feet by twelve-feet it's the smallest church in England.

Clever academics think the Culbone stone was nicked from the ancient row and placed beside an old Dark Age track to become a guide for travellers to the tiny settlement. Obviously, locals would know where the church was, so perhaps the slanted stem was a 'spypost fer furriners'.

Aboard the Land Rover once more, Mark and I took the tortuous, boneshaking, multi-gated farm track downhill, following the four o'clock line as best we could into the valley.

In the days before the mystical mists became the reserve of Glastonbury, another player of the harmonium, the American psychologist Joan D'Arcy Cooper, came to Culbone. However, unlike the exhibitions of the notorious Miss Bom-Bane previously alluded to, Joan's performances were certainly not of the funky kind and were exclusive to the keyboard in St Beuno's church. She was eccentric in another way.

A sepia photograph portrays Joan as a rather pensive character with a 'Christopher Robin' haircut. Yet, as a nature-mystic, yogi and an Ascended Mistress of the Rainbow Programme, whatever that was, Joan was clearly a slightly alternative if not colourful lady who believed that we are never alone. "Our individual guardian angel," she wrote, "accompanies us throughout our life on Earth."

She was the wife of the famous artist potter Waistel Cooper, formerly of Reykjavik and Porlock, and lived at Keeper's Lodge down by the stream in Culbone where her husband established a studio in the 1950s. It was here that Waistel started using a kick-wheel and installed an oil-fired kiln. He could well have been a notable painter rather than a notable potter. But fate intervened in the shape of a sculptor friend, "It was a strange happening, but from the first moment I put my hands in clay I was hooked." In Culbone, Waistel's potting blossomed, his pots getting simpler and more focused, and his reputation grew. His mark was the brushed forename 'Waistel' in black. "With such a forename," he often said, "I hardly need a surname." Today his pots are the stuff of wealthy collectors.

For her part, Joan was a licensed 'Reader' in the diocese of Bath and Wells and a much sought after spiritual healer, which isn't surprising given Culbone's location. Her income, though, came by writing, being a part-time freelance psychologist and using her own methods to teach yoga, relaxation, and meditation for West Somerset Community Education. Upon her death in the summer of 1982, she was buried in Culbone churchyard.

She lies close by a gravestone that reads:

> "To the memory of
> John Red
> of this parish who departed
> in the year of our Lord 1852.
> in the 70th year of his sage."

I thought at the time of reading it that this was a grand age for sage. The stuff in my herb bed has barely lasted a quarter dozen years.

Joan is almost an odd one out in a churchyard filled with the local names not just of Red but also of Richards; two families that became joined through marriage by Richard Red Richards, an award winning Vale of Porlock malt-barley farmer who's buried amongst the lot of them.

However, what interested me about Joan were her delves into local history. She traced the origins of a small stone window a chancel window of two lights, cut in a single stone and embossed with a wild boar in St Bueno's chancel, back to a chiselling Saxon age eremitic monk. The window pointed me in the right direction to unearth a fascinating past to a place that had a history of banishment.

As a younger man in straw hat and linen jacket aping the age of *Brideshead Revisited* I heard tales of Culbone. High stone walls, spooky tunnels and gothic towers in the shadow of rhododendrons lined the woodland path that led from the white wicket gate at Porlock's toll house. I was told they were built to keep lepers in, but I was misinformed. They were in fact the remains of walls and follies of an Italianate garden created two hundred years ago at Ashleigh Combe for Ada, Countess of Lovelace the only legitimate daughter of Lord Byron. Indeed, the steep and bumpy Worthy toll road owes its very existence to Ada as it was built to give access to the romantic house her husband Lord King built as a home for her that's now overgrown and hidden in the dark woods.

And like the woods, Culbone's history, too, was dark. Virtually until the end of the seventeenth century, the place had been known as Kitnor. And before that 'K'sh'b'h', which when spoken probably sounded like an incredulous cough. Over time Culbone became home to social nuisances, then oddly, some Bengalis from East India and, of course, the lepers. All were subjected to old-fashioned values of community care.

It's a past that began, to my mind, in 1280, the date Thomas, the chaplain of Culbone, found himself in hot water. Before that the place was almost deserted. The Assize rolls say that Thomas 'had struck Albert of Esshe on the head with a hatchet, and so killed him'. Esshe was the old name for Ash so perhaps Thomas was merely rekindling an old friendship or cutting Albert down to size.

Theirs was the time when Culbone had become a place to where men, women and children thought a social nuisance by local priests were banished. Atheists, witches and the potty all qualified. Nothing was provided for them. Allowed no visitors and only their personal possessions, they were left to fend for themselves. However, the motley crowd did a good job building stone huts, growing food, making their own clothes and nursing the sick. Some even taught the children. Just occasionally a priest, such as Thomas, would make sure no one had gone AWOL.

A hundred years on, and it was men only. Culbone became a temporary gaol for ninety-three years. Thieves and adulterers were sent there with sentences ranging from a matter of months to over five years. Separated from their families, and with never more than nineteen blokes for company at any time, some went mad, or killed themselves in despair. Their only solace offered to them was a once a month service in St Beuno's. Being forced to attend it, though, probably only embittered them more.

By the middle of the sixteenth century it was all change again – the first lepers arrived. They were males and females of all ages suffering this most unpleasant of chronic human conditions caused by the bacteria *Mycobacterium leprae* and *Mycobacterium lepromatosis*. Left untreated as it was, leprosy was progressive, causing permanent damage to the skin, nerves, limbs and eyes. Contrary to myth, leprosy didn't cause body parts to fall off but rightly believing leprosy to be contagious the Church and the civil authorities in their wisdom decided to create Exmoor's only leper colony. There was the considerable fear that the disease was spreading in England.

The lepers themselves were left as outcasts without care of any kind. Yes, they were given seed but no tools or implements so they were forced to forage for food. Shelter was rudimentary, the lepers having to do their best with the ruins of the old stone huts. And so it was for seventy-eight years during which the colony was recorded as living 'in simple dignity'. The tiny 'leper window' seen today that's constructed in the north wall of the church was only there for reasons of tradition to emphasize that lepers could never receive the Eucharist. During the time of the lepers a hermit lived in isolation and prayer for fifteen years in a tiny cell within the church until his death.

The last batch of people banished to Culbone were rather exotic - a group of Bengali men who spoke very little English. They had the misfortune of being taken prisoner by the British in India, used as servants, and eventually brought back to England. Surplus to requirements as servants, thirty-eight of them were sent to Culbone in 1730 to work as charcoal burners long before summer barbecues made such endeavour fashionable.

On the Bengalis' arrival services ceased being held in the church so they maintained the building for use as a communal dwelling and kitchen. From time to time small boats came up the coast to take away the charcoal that had been burnt in Yarner woods. In exchange the Bengalis were given sugar and Indian tea. This was an age ahead of local entrepreneur Derek Miles seeing the potential of establishing his successful tea merchant business in Porlock.

After twenty-one years the Bengalis were allowed their freedom. Something that I presume the powers-that-be thought was a damned decent gesture. Unfortunately, fifteen Bengalis had died in the interim and none of the survivors was ever able to return to India.

Within fifty years of the Bengalis' departure Sam Coleridge and Will Hazlitt made their first visits to Culbone and thereafter it became a place for romantics. Certainly, Sam was moved to wax lyrical:

> "But oh! that deep romantic chasm which slanted
> Down the green hill athwart a cedarn cover!
> A savage place! as holy and enchanted
> As e'er beneath a waning moon was haunted
> By woman wailing for her demon-lover!"

Culbone was put on the map. It even got a pub. A year before St Beuno's became decorated with its small steeple in 1822, one of the hamlet's six cottages began calling itself the Fox and Hounds and remained open for over five and a half decades.

A lichen rich and mossy gravestone in St Beuno's poignantly, although perhaps unwittingly, sums up Culbone's past better than Sam's lines:

> "In
> Memory of
> Mary Bromham, who died.
> Novr. 1st. 1820. aged 86 years.
> O. happy change - my God has set me free.
> From this vain world and all its misery."

The small stone window embossed with a wild boar has had a lot of faces gaze through it. Clambering back into the Land Rover I wondered how many would have believed Joan D'Arcy Cooper that they had a guardian angel looking after them.

SIXTEEN

Trees of Stone

"Is it elf, is it gnome, is it fairy
The form no one perceives?
I remember: nothing was there.
I feel, and yearning believes."
Fernando Pessoa, Portuguese poet and writer, 1888 -1933.

Chocolate eggs packed in gaudy cardboard and plastic were anathema to the Romanians who greeted one another other: "Christos a-nviat" meaning "Christ has arisen". They searched Minehead supermarket shelves for food colourings to colour the shells of their hardboiled eggs. "Cu adevarat a-nviat," that's to say "He has truly arisen", came the traditional reply as vital ingredients like Savoy cabbage for 'sarmale' and semolina for 'supa cu galuste' were ticked off with relief on shopping lists. These were the horse handlers and the pig slaughterers, and those that farm laboured or worked long hours at local hotels, Butlins and Maccy D. And for them it was Easter in a foreign country.

As if opening the dock gates of Porlock Weir's rude harbour, hearing the language opened a flood of memory of an Easter recently past when, in the Moldovan capital city of Chisinau, I was introduced by my interpreter to Radu, a Moldovan who was an acclaimed Moscow trained energy healer. In his basement consulting room, Radu told me to eat less pork and then he lit a candle. Looking into the flame, he gave me the reassurance I sought in a time of emotion. "Your father has gone to a good place," he said.

"Mool-tsoo-mesk, (Thank you)" I responded.

"Cu placere. (You're welcome)"

A week later I was in Monksilver, my Dad's home village. It was poignant he had chosen to live in a former cloth making parish given that his forebears manufactured fabric in England's north country. In the Domesday Book the place had simply been Selvre, from the Latin silva for a wood, and so today folk assume the name means 'monk's wood'. However, in the 890s it was known as Sulfhere, after the stream called the Silver that burbles through the village.

All in all it's a soporific locale of nasty road bends, a new-ish village hall oddly chosen as a venue for HGV driver courses, thatched roofed extremely expensive housing stock, oodles of pensioners, one of whom, Anne, escaped from Palestine during the war rolled up in Persian carpet, and the Notley Arms pub from which its debt ridden landlord, a former Zimbabwean farmer, recently did a night runner leaving behind enlarged photos of zebras pulling hay carts. I just hoped the clandestine departure had nothing to do with my Dad and his muckers chuckling about the 'silver' at the bottom of their gardens making them good for credit whenever they asked to have their pints put on bar tabs.

For other regulars, a Jack Russell and a Yorkshire terrier, the news had been most spirit dampening. Suddenly overnight they were deprived of their privilege of having a bar stool each on which to park their bottoms as long as they sat beside their respective masters. The term 'lap dogs' had had a very different meaning when applied to the pair of canine wagtails. Dogs, my Granny once said, have the power of seeing death as it approaches. And there was me taking the expression in the eyes of the hairy bar-stoolers being just for want of sharing my bacon-flavoured crisps.

This was my thought knowing that day I hadn't come to Monksilver to bibble. Far from it. Instead, I was there for a memorial service in All Saints church renowned for its extremely rare Easter sepulchre, an arched recess in which the crucifix and sacred elements commemorating Christ's entombment and resurrection were placed between Good Friday and Easter Day. Such a sepulchre is unique to England with the practice belonging to the Sarum Rite established by Saint Osmund, Bishop of Salisbury in the eleventh century.

However, the sepulchre was empty of artefacts when I stood on the chancel step facing a sea of faces filling the church nave. Folk had come from far afield as well as drifting in from more local homes. A pew-silent awkward audience doing what they felt was right, paying their respects. Courteous listeners to the eulogy I spoke about my Dad. But I was soon to be reminded of the words of George Ade, an American journo, who was really quite perceptive when he said: "In the city a funeral is just an interruption of traffic; in the country it is a form of popular entertainment."

Inadvertently, my left foot trod on a thin gas pipe. My downward pressure was enough to trigger a leg nerve into uncontrollable spasm making me appear to all and sundry that I must be a sufferer of Saint Vitus dance.

But this was All Saints after all and it had featured in a story I had once written that got read on the radio. It was about how a Monksilver blacksmith helped himself to some fairy gold, and for his pains was turned by magic into a gruesome pig-beast whose likeness remains preserved as a grotesque hunky punk sitting beside another that seems to represent a tooth extraction. The blacksmith's tools, I claimed, could be seen today, immortalised in one of the church's stained glass windows. Of course it was all twaddle. The window merely depicted the Arma Christi - the objects associated with Jesus' Passion in a church Easter obsessed.

As I tried not to jiggle on that chancel step I could see the window out of the corner of my eye – a further distraction to my talk of Dad's brown felt hat, his love of growing sweet peas, his propensity for dark silences and of his having a secret past of which he never spoke.

Later, after the post church vol-au-vents, dire wine and compassion of strangers, I found some old photographs and papers in a small battered box amongst Dad's personal effects. Here were Second World War memories of cholera and of discovering prisoners of war that were far less amusing than any Persian carpet story. I felt that I hadn't done him justice and remembered a story about a man scattering sand from a bag that he carried. "Why are you scattering that sand?" an onlooker asked.

"It's magic sand to keep dragons away," the man replied.

"But there are no dragons here," remarked the onlooker.

"You see," said the man; "it works."

Like the man who scattered sand we all have a need to believe in something to escape the reality of both the present and the memory of which we cannot speak. Even to those we love. I never felt that I knew Dad other than as a man of silence. And it had become a silence that after a heart transplant I had been learning, too.

A tad self-indulgent perhaps, I took it upon myself to make a short film that I called *Tree of Dragons*. The film followed my journey to comprehend Dad's silences that affected me as a child and caused me to escape into the sanctuary of nature immersing myself in the romance of superstition and a world of make-belief. Needing both closure and catharsis I found inspiration in Exmoor's venerable history after rapidly laid travel plans had taken me first to India and then to the Thai-Burmese border where Dad had been traumatised by cruelties beside the River Kwai. On a train journey alongside that river I, too, found silence and came to understand that some things are best kept to oneself like the wartime deaths of friends or my own internal dragons of suffering.

By his actions Man has a tendency to be disturbing. Photographs taken from the air over Exmoor proves the obvious in a mundane way. Peat cuttings, quarries and smidgen traces of past army training litter the moor. But from the upheavals of the earth also arose the evocative.

Standing stones caught my boyhood imagination - those like Culbone stone row, stone circles on Withypool Hill and Porlock Common near the bridge over Colley Water and the Caractacus Stone on Winsford Hill. These are the true ancients from a time when a bank wasn't something that sent nasty letters, a barrow couldn't be pushed and Man erected stones to resemble the trees that made mockery of a mortal life span. Long stones at Beaple's Hill, and West Anstey are goodly examples, once ideal for getting bearings in the days before GPS.

Yet of all Exmoor's tall stones, the grey, weather-worn, lichen crusted, Challacombe Longstone, high on the spine of the moor is quite literally the most outstanding. Stood one-and-a-half times my height on the boggy spring-line of the clear amber water of the River Bray that in a while turned into the Mole, for me this was my tree of dragons. And it was kept company by splendid specimens of burial mounds, the Chapman Barrows, from which Victorians and Edwardians unearthed such delights as internment pits, inverted urns, charcoal and bone ash.

Writing his *Stag Hunting on Exmoor* in the 1880s John Fortescue described the landscape perfectly as "a plain of red and yellow grass patched with black pits full of rich brown peaty water, tangled tufts of rushes, mats of warm green moss; a paradise for snipe. To our right are a few mounds or barrows, one especially higher, broader, and rounder than the rest. Mount on the top and say what you can see all round you, for this lonely spot shows the finest view in Exmoor. The whole of North Devon is spread out before you like a map."

And it was to this once sacred place that I set out, a couple of months after my chancel dancing, to record key images for my film. On a rare day that Challacombe didn't seem to merit its 'cold valley' meaning I had swallowed an antihistamine and armed myself with my brasher hiking stick, tripod and backpack of camera kit. And having gained lunchtime sustenance of cider and a chunky roast pork sandwich at the Black Venus I took the path from lonely Whitefield Barton farm that leads up, down and up and over Challacombe Common to Holwell Castle and Parracombe.

But I wasn't going all the way, only as far as the ridge where a rickety wooden gate in a beech hedge opened to Chapman Barrows. Emerging at the top of the first down bit by some crow feathers, across the valley I saw the Longstone as a tiny sentinel caught in sunshine and heard the first cuckoo of the year.

Sight and sound made me almost skip downwards between rocks and fern bouncing away energy, something I soon regretted as I yomped steeply up to the ridge gate. Once through it I simply followed my boots towards the Longstone. Although Fortescue was right about the views, I saw no sign of snipe that were most probably in hiding from the sound of my breathless wheezing. Or more likely from the cacophonous roar of low flying R.A.F. jets suddenly playing silly buggers and spooking a herd of grazing red deer hinds and a couple of stags in velvet. Breeze blown pollen floated ad nauseum past my eyes and I found the Longstone standing bog-dry in a sea of fluffy headed cotton grass. Oh, joyous rendezvous.

A few good folk surmised Man worshipped 'Trees of Stone' root-reaching to the dragon earth mother, and that important healing was in the hands of the shaman who retrieved stolen souls. A world of spirit behind closed eyelid dark. A world of so many stories becoming the tenets of belief.

In *Tree of Dragons* I had asked questions: heart transplanted and mind fearful, does the spirit of my donor need retrieving from me? Can the soul of my birth heart be returned by medicine of the mind? It was heavy stuff. I saw dragons as creatures of my mind's imaginings. Given life by the stories I write as my escape from yearning for the soul part that is missing. Cut away, leaving body failing fears.

Certainly, the healing gifts of shamans existed before the Danish Vikings made their raids on the Exmoor coast at Porlock and Watchet, bringing with them their talk of the sisters Urd, Verdandi, and Skuld the three spinners who wove fate beneath the mythological giant ash tree of Yggdrasil as four deer representing the four winds ran through its branches. Those spinners began to weave the destiny of the world around the period the Royal Forest first came into being. This had to raise the question whether they had foreseen the local legend being created of Alfred holding the nearby square earthwork of Shoulsbury Castle against their mortal believers.

However, the Vikings were Scandinavian latecomers compared to the Maglemosian immigrants from Denmark whose burins, flint tools used for cutting antler or bone, were found at Doniford. Arriving to the Exmoor fringe four thousand years ago, Heaven knows what they believed in as it was an age before the erection of the Challacombe Longstone was even contemplated.

When I got round to explaining away my fascination of menhirs to my wife she had looked at me quizzically. "Mènières," she said, "What's so great about tinnitus and recurrent attacks of earth spinning vertigo?"

I quickly reassured her that I wasn't hooked on a disease but that my interest was just in Bronze Age shamanism. My wife almost seemed impressed. "I never knew you were so esoteric," she said, and whilst turning the kettle on, added "Make yourself useful."

So I blew the cat hairs off my laptop, and with a sneeze began tapping out a story.

The Itchy-Eyed Dragon of Challacombe

Dragons were as rare as Exmoor silver and to Tulla the Wise just as precious. To everyone else dragons were a pain, particularly on sun-hot days when flowers and grasses filled the air with pollen. And so it was with Black Venus, a passing dragon who came to stay.

Where the River Barle has its source in the shallow bog above Challacombe there is a Longstone, the tallest on the moor. A sacred place where stone age people worshipped water gods and cremated their loved ones. The bone ash of the important was scooped into urns that were buried either side of the Longstone within great barrow mounds. Mounds that lined the spine of the moor. They were visible from far away and caught a dragon's streaming eye as it flew by one summer's day.

What a perfect place for a dribbly dragon to lay its weary head. A barrow mound for a pillow. Boggy squelchiness sun-dried to a spongy bed to stretch out upon and soothe a tired scaly-hard ebony body. Cool spring water bubbling to soak the throat and slake the thirst. Wandering deer and pasturing sheep were plentiful to nab and chew. There was even that Longstone to scratch those terrible itches. Small wonder the dragon flopped a barbed tail from side to side in the bliss of relief.

A few brave men came to grunt their disapproval and poke the crotchety creature with stone tipped spears, only to become bone-ash sooner than they had hoped when the dragon opened its mouth wide, sneezed and frazzled them in flame. No, it wasn't good to get too close to a hayfevered dragon with a runny nose.

"Shnaah-thooo! Shnaah-thooo!" The dragon's sneezes echoed in the combe and about Swincombe rocks, the home of Tulla the Wise.

For many summers Tulla had come to sit beside the longstone, caring not a jot for burial mounds and potted charcoaled bones, but believing in the will of the gods. Stroking hare-tails of cotton grass across the palm of her hand. Enjoying the solitude. Seeking omens in the clouds and in feathers on the ground. Then came the day of sneezing sound. On the ridge of barrows Tulla had seen smoke-grey clouds. Red deer skedaddled. Skylarks rose in flutters of anxiety, crows cawed, and feathers spun and twirled to litter the earth. To Tulla it could only be the coming of the gods. She dressed in her finest deerskin, ran her fingers through her hair and set off up the combe to greet them.

Tulla met no gods, but instead found a pathetic limp-winged dragon rubbing red watery eyes on the rounded tip of the Longstone. Rubbing and rubbing. Tulla's mouth opened and let out a gasp at the sight of the dark scorch marks, bits of charcoal and charred stone-tipped spears. The dragon turned its head towards her, blind blinking through tears.

Hiding her fear Tulla spoke softly to the dragon which merely groaned, turning attention from rubbing its itchy blood-shot eyes to rubbing its itchy dripping nose. Dragon-scales chafed in frenzy at the Longstone's edge. Then the sniffly beast sneezed again. "Shnaah-thooo!…Shnaah-thooo!…SHNAAH-THOOO!!"

Snout thrown flame followed snout thrown flame to sizzle out in the dragon-drenched mire, enshrouding Tulla in hot mists of steam. She fell backwards onto her backside in shock, flattening a patch of moorland grass, causing pollen to drift about her face. Her eyes began to prick and she rubbed instinctively. Then Tulla understood and her fears ceased; instead she felt only sympathy for the poor thing.

Taking care to stand behind the dragon's snout, Tulla turned her face to the clouds and whispered to the water-gods. Greyness gathered overhead, closing out the sun in a stilled world turning dark dimpsey. Tulla raised her arms outstretched above her head and cried out imploringly.

The lightning flash was sudden. The thunderclap was louder than any dragon-sneeze. The rain torrential. Tulla danced in gladness. Splashing about the Longstone that now stood in a deepening of sopping bog. Flowers and grasses bent heavy with sodden pollen. The dragon had gained relief.

Days passed. The nose dried and bloodshot eyes turned bright, each as bright as the brightest night star. Tulla the wise named the dragon Black Venus. For years before her spirit became free Tulla would summon the rains when flowers bloomed and grasses turned to seed, up upon that high place where once again dragons may sneeze. Up where the hair-tailed cotton grass grows at the source of the River Bray, Tulla's ash remains possibly lie buried within one of the last barrow mounds. The one the dragon was to adopt as a pillow till the end of its days. A dragon whose legacy is left on the Longstone where the lower half thins; that gentle curve caused by summer rubbing of an itchy nose.

SEVENTEEN

Epicurean Paddlers

"You know well that the otter has greater wisdom than a man."
Iroquois Indian proverb.

The sun was shining, the primroses were out, the teetsy-totsies had joined them, and I entered Mike Thorne's award winning Wivey butcher's shop intent on buying more slices of the best ham in Christendom and a half dozen local eggs with flavour divine. Ahead of me at the counter was my neighbour Gill. Having unwisely let on to spending years producing radio programmes for the BBC at London's Bush House she had been 'volunteered' as a presenter for our local 10Radio station serving ten parishes. But she epitomised the spirit hereabouts of the alternative economy in the face of recessionary crisis. And indeed, exchanging a book for an oven ready skinny chicken or a sack of damp logs was not unknown to me.

"'Otter days are 'ere again,'" said Gill as we exchanged morning pleasantries. With International Women's Day come and gone I knew she had been among ladies of a certain age complaining that it had been a little chilly in the Community Hall for the belly dancing session.

"They've come a bit late, haven't they?" I said trying to sound consoling. If I touched a nerve, Gill didn't show it.

Still holding on to the belly dancing vision I then thought she said something about herself interviewing an Ottoman and being reluctant to ask him about

Frogs. A Turk with die-hard tendencies I could understand, but it was most unlike liberal minded Gill to be disparaging about the French.

However, when she dropped in the name 'Mister Spraint', my mist of misapprehension cleared. She was on about James who had gained himself a reputation for being 'the otter man' due to his acquired knowledge of *lutra lutra* and through what the *Spectator* called his rather heavy didactic book *The Otter Among Us*. Now he was a major spokesman for the Somerset Otter Group.

Apart from dawn surface ripples, a wet nose twitch and an eye glint at Landacre Bridge I have only seen local otters once and that was in the glare of my headlights on a country lane a pheasant glide from the Batherm. An adult and a couple of cubs had bowled along in front of my bonnet for a short distance in the manner often adopted by squirrels before they vanished into the night through a farm gate. From that moment I realised otters can charm to the point of inspiring devotion. It was easy to lose the focus of their being not only the largest predator upon Exmoor but in Britain in general, so I could understand someone wanting to speak up for them.

I had come across good man James by accident not long ago while he was leading a training session on 'otter spotting' to a straggling gaggle of attentive devotees along the banks of the River Barle near the Wheal Eliza, the long dormant riverside mine worked for miserable return first for copper between 1845 and 1854 and then for iron ore until 1857.

Within two years after its closure the mine's return became even more miserable when it was pumped dry with the purpose of finding Anna-Maria Burgess. Find her they did. Her corpse was at the bottom of the shaft, hidden there by her father William. Convicted of his daughter's murder he was hanged at Taunton in retribution for Exmoor's most horrible crime. The otter fanciers' appearance put an end to my quiet pursuit of filming a heron that flapped languidly away with sonorous croaks.

Detached from the main bunch I saw two wildlife buffs having a conflab over something of interest that was lying in the molinia grass. Inquisitiveness got the better of me and found that they were staring at what can be best described as a white blob of gloop.

"Wow! Amazing! It's an otter's anal jelly!" exclaimed a young woman in dungarees.

"Oh, rubbish," responded a lank-haired lad wearing spectacles. "There's only one thing that it could be and that's stag semen."

I bent down and ultra scientifically poked the gloop with my finger. "Could be celestial snot from a meteorite. Since the seventeenth century poets have called the stuff 'Star Jelly'." I said it as a guess, and got a pair of indignant looks to suggest I was in no way part of their gang.

But to be honest the substance really was quite curious, enough so for me to take some camera footage to play back later to a 'friend-that-knows'. The buffs wanted to show James then and there but he had moved on round a river bend. Still deep in discussion the buffs trotted to catch up and I for a while tagged on eavesdropping on the health and safety aspects of otter surveying. I realised we now lived in a world completely lacking in common sense.

James gave every indication of being a wannabe Henry Williamson, a chap who loved a coke and a wedging as is the way with those familiar with their otter droppings. Dedicated, clean shaven and turned grey by over thirty years as schoolmaster in Somerset, James appeared prim and proper in green wellies and grey windcheater, poking at what looked like poo on a river rock with the tip of what I mistook to be a 'Robin Hood' stave, but was in reality a two metre long polished pole, the traditional preserve of the old otter hunter. As if to prove the point James named the faecal deposit 'otter spraint' with total conviction. I offered the facetious suggestion that the offending stool might alternatively have been laid by a paddling Brobdingnagian stoat and met with the humourless derision reserved for the classroom dunce.

I beat a hasty retreat, wishing that I had sensibly argued the possible presence of mink.

If James had been Williamson he might just have thrown an apple at me in the way Henry used to do in the 1920s to passers-by when he wasn't swimming naked, writing *Tarka the Otter* at Skirr Cottage in Georgeham, or following the Cheriton Otter Hounds whose oldest pack pooch at that time was 'Dreamy'. Out of interest, Henry, didn't feel 'Dreamy' sounded baleful enough for his purposes, so in *Tarka* he gave the chief hound another name – Deadlock.

Otter hunting stopped voluntarily many years ago when the huntsmen noticed a fall in otter numbers. This fall was nothing to do with hunting but as a result of environmental nasties. But I've often thought it a courteous touch that Henry dedicated his famous book to William Rogers the Master of the Cheritons. He and his fellows had been a smart bunch dressed in white breeches, white stock, dark blue cloth coats and waistcoats, pale grey 'pot hats' or bowlers and heavy boots. Their long polished poles were incised with cuts denoting various kills. Thankfully I didn't see any such notches on James's poo prodding pole.

A survey done twenty years ago by the Devon Wildlife Trust and the Somerset Trust for Nature Conservation revealed that otters had virtually vanished from Exmoor. There was only scarce evidence of breeding, and such otters as still existed or might have padded into Exmoor were too few to perpetuate themselves. But now, protected by the Wildlife and Countryside Act, the otter is up there with the secretive grasshopper warbler, distinctive for its whirring song rather than its leaps of faith, in making an Exmoor comeback. By colonising their old haunts again they appear to be kicking out the mink, but sadly too late to save the water vole, Ratty in *Wind in the Willows*, mink-gobbled to Exmoor extinction.

Evidence of otter return sits on my study bookshelf. *Stormforce - An Otter's Tale* written by David Chaffe at the end of the '90s is a true story about Storm, an otter bitch, rescued weighing just one pound seven ounces from an Exmoor lane one winter's dawn by a kindly postman. The book is the remarkable story of the otter's survival to become a TV star appearing on ITV's Survival *The Wensum Year* and the BBC Natural History Unit's *Living Britain* and *Otters, the Truth*. It was so much easier to ask Storm nicely rather than try to encourage the occupant of any old holt to perform in front of a large camera lens and a microphone suited in a fluffy windjammer, alarmingly resembling a rigor mortised rabbit.

David regularly gave lectures with Storm at Hinkley Point Visitor Centre. The basic message of his talks was very simple: to survive, the otter needs the same three conditions as humans – a secure home, a supply of food and clean water. It was David's belief that Storm's mum made her way onto Exmoor by way of one of the many streams that flow into the Bristol Channel close to the nuclear power station.

Then, in 2002, conclusive evidence of growing otter numbers was shown, scientists opined, by finds of legless dead frogs at Westermill Farm near Exford. It had been a slaughter of hundreds. Although otters mostly feed on fish, crunchy crabs, waterfowl and amphibians are also on the menu. Of the latter, with a toad being as unpalatable to an otter as a vole is to my cat, frogs provide the tastiest choice, well, at least their legs do. In Exmoor circles the otter deserves to compete with the red legged partridge for the title of 'Little Frenchman'.

Frogs have fairly toxic skin. Otters are sensible enough to remove the legs and skin them, to get at the inside morsels of meat. Notoriety for such epicurean behaviour resulted in the farmer of Westermill, Oliver Edwards, being interviewed by the BBC. Otters were in his bad books. "I was very concerned, because the otters wiping out our frogs," he reportedly said. "We like to see small frogs and all the other things that go with conservation areas. To wipe out the frog population in the food chain is not very good. I'm glad that the otters are here and long may it last, but I'm not so happy that they are eating my frogs."

Happily otters have behaved themselves better elsewhere, and hearsay has it that they have been received with open arms in Tarr Woods now owned by the National Park Authority. Here their 'presence' helped the oak clothed woods clinging to steep rocky valley slopes be recognised as being of National Nature Reserve standard, one of the highest nature conservation accolades. Perhaps the otters were attracted to a weird glow-in-the-dark moss that can found in burrows amongst the trees or maybe just wanted to provide company for rare barbastelle bats.

Whatever drew the otters they have to contend with the grockle hordes that descend on the 'honey-pot' that's Tarr Steps bringing with them floundering retrievers and splashing spaniels or, as I witnessed, a sinking pekinese. The bedraggled, hairy rat-thing was only saved by being washed bankwards towards its hysterical, screaming mistress by Richard Growden's Exmoor Safari Land Rover as it churned the Barle waters while crossing the river alongside the ancient clapper bridge. All the otters can do is gawp at lesser aquatic creatures and grumble at the disturbances caused to their fish suppers, or go elsewhere.

Indeed, one can only cogitate that it could have been a Tarr otter that had taken to the Tarka trail, the bit that runs from Exe head to Pinkery Pond and on to Wood Barrow before heading off to Brayford. The usual territory of an otter is about eleven miles, although distances of twenty-five have been recorded, but this is all to do with the density of food availing itself.

Paul Madgett, one of James's 'Otter Spotters' had photographed an otter footprint in the snows of last winter whilst walking near that laboured result of Irish navvies, Pinkery Pond. By following the animal's paw prints Paul concluded that it had been a visitor to the exploration centre. Obviously, the otter was seeking up-to-date information of the whereabouts of itself and its fellows.

Better that it wasn't told to check out the Royal Oak in Withypool where at lunchtime a multitude of muddied and sweat-pongy walking boot pairs more often than not lie hugger-mugger by the threshold door. Over a pint of prawns I had made mental notes of the age-worn trophies of stuffed, glassy-eyed heads, hooves and paws of stag, fox, and most poignantly, otter mounted on wall hung wooden plaques. This was the village once tended by a Dodo, well, that's the name a forester had recorded in the Domesday Book, and R.D. Blackmore, having got intimate knowledge of Exmoor when it was his youthful stamping ground, is rumoured to have written some pages of *Lorna Doone* at the pub's bar. Perhaps they were those that spoke of the Lyn where 'an otter might float downstream likening himself to a log of wood, with his flat head flush with the water-top, and his oily eyes peering quietly; and yet no panic would seize other life, as it does when a sample of man comes', or maybe the bit about Lorna's hair coming down, "in a way to be remembered, upon the left and fairest part" of John Ridd's favourite otter-skin waistcoat.

However, the pub displays a framed letter of non committal written by R.D.B. dated July 10th 1866 from his Teddington home in London addressed to the then landlord Mr Warner: "It will give me great pleasure to be with you (if possible) at the time you mention. But I am so terribly pressed this week that I cannot be certain of the pleasure." So whether or not R.D.B did actually turn up in Withypool with pen and paper is open to conjecture. And with Lynmouth's Rising Sun and Porlock's Ship making similar claims to playing host to his scribbling, the writer, through no fault of his own, has gained the reputation of being a role model for a pub crawler.

During the 1930s a subsequent landlord was to become the focus of tittle-tattle. Maxwell Knight, the spymaster and radio broadcaster, upon whom Ian Fleming based his character 'M', James Bond's boss, ran the pub with his wife, Gwladys. Weirdly, she died in London's Overseas Visitors Club after some sort of occult misadventure involving Aleister Crowley, the notorious MI5 agent, code-named 'The Great Beast' and heroin-addicted, Satan worshipping, Dark Lord of Tarot.

As I consigned this to memory together with the fact of some saying General

Eisenhower drank cider in the Royal Oak whilst planning the invasion of Normandy, a young girl looking about five or six was a bit perturbed and tugged a parental hand as she stared upwards at the assembly of inanimate fauna. "Daddy, are those animals dead? I don't want them to be dead," she said.

Not wanting possible attention drawing tears, her father, distracting himself from cidrous desire and the bar menu, seemed to be a quick thinker. "No sweetheart, they're not dead they're being statue artists like the gold painted man you saw in Taunton standing still for hours and hours before he lifted his top hat. If you could see behind the wall I'm sure that otter would wiggle its bum for you."

"'Don't be silly, Daddy. Can I have sausage and chips?"

As Gill was leaving the butcher's I called after her: "I dare you to ask Mister Spraint if he's ever actually seen a live Exmoor otter in the wild or just those preserved by taxidermy."

"Heavens, no. It'd be more than my life's worth."

"Then please ask him about frogs."

"No!"

"Anal jelly?"

"Absolutely not!" And there were Gill's final words as she closed the door on the topic until faced by the 10Radio studio microphone in an interview that failed to have questions answered. And to be honest, on the subject matter of gloop neither were mine.

Jonathan Farey, a farming friend, said he would have loved it be stag semen because he had seen something remarkably similar on top of his rusty red tractor. Just to be boring he thought it bog standard bacteria jelly. Taking further advice, however, the consensus was that it was either the result of slugs freezing and exploding or the result of herons regurgitating frogs. For the sake of peace of mind I settled on the latter. All things considered, as an answer it seemed the most fitting as I couldn't bring myself to believe such an epicurean paddler as an otter would pass anything other than frogs legs in aspic.

EIGHTEEN

Ribbons, Buns and Pneumatics

"All music is folk music. I ain't never heard a horse sing a song."
Louis Armstrong, American jazz trumpeter and singer, 1901 – 1971.

Cute they might be but Malmesmead's barking Muntjac deer having gorged on primroses were eyeing up the bluebells and for added flavour that garlic substitute, Jack by the hedge. Somerset's cricketers blinked to find themselves bottom of the infant championship table. Soon the early-purple orchids would flower.

Handyman Ian Wigley, hubby of the organiser of the Golden Horseshoe, gave a spruce-up to the giant MDF horseshoe he had constructed for Exford's start and finish of the hundred mile event that taxed horses and riders. Gymkhana season had commenced with tears, tantrums and bad language, taxing all concerned. And with the dust beginning to settle over stories of Icelandic volcanic ash clouds there were dark horses elsewhere with the way clear for election fever.

According to the Minehead Bun-o-Meter the squished whort blues led the blood reds with both the custard yellows and healthy greens trailing badly. For the fifth general election running baker Steve Wells had made his party pieces of iced buns in the colours of the four main political persuasions. In reality it was nice of him to even bother. The reds these days don't bother breaking sweat hereabouts. Conceding early to failure in what by all accounts was a two horse race, they looked to brown pastures east of Frome.

Perhaps they tended to forget Ernest Bevin the famous Labour Foreign Secretary was born in Winsford in 1881, the seventh child of Diana Bevin, more affectionately known as Mercy, who was separated from her husband by the time Ernest was born. Then again, Ernest's firm anti-communism almost made him a whort worthy. So much so that Lenin Court, a London housing project designed by a Russian émigré architect, Berthold Lubetkin in the early 1940s, was renamed Bevin Court in Ernest's honour.

I learned from Winsford-born Ken Baker, a sadly now dead gardener-chauffeur-butler who loved the bluebells in Burrow Wood, that his stonemason dad went to school with Ernest and it was he who put up the plaque about him. Ken, locally famous himself for his decades old Morris Traveller with low mileage caused by the amount of time he spent running with the hunt aided by hanging on to passing stirrups, was too young to know the great man. Yet, as a child he was aware of Ernest's cousins living next door.

By way of gossip Ken said it was reckoned Ernest 'came across the fields' and that David Evans the Royal Oak's landlord was the daddy. Mercy worked as a cleaner in the pub and guilt was 'proven' by David not sticking around. Just think, without his help there would have been no 'Bevin Boys' saying "mine, mine, mine". And for what it's worth, the thatched cottage where Ernest drew first breath was later owned, when the village became more refined, by my old school headmaster Mr Crabbe. But let me not get distracted by debate.

In Wivey's Skoda Row, I had my own insight into the state of the canvass. Having discovered green fungus growing on my summer shoes stored in the damp under-stairs cupboard I considered them rank outsiders whichever way I looked at it.

The starlings in the eaves decided that mimicking Toffee the long-haired dachshund was now passé as she had moved to Cornwall. The new chihuahua the other side of my garden wall was now the rat-pooch of preference.

"Yap-yap, yap-yap" shrieked the starlings. It was a good game and they deserved ten out of ten for interpretation. A pair of great tits sang "teacher, teacher" at the ringleader. The best acrobats in the local talent show the tits were also prone to proudly say 'chink' on the lip of their wall hole between the garden's pink-blossomed apple tree and the silver birch whose seeds had floated annoyingly in their hundreds through every open window. They accompanied the multitudes of feathery parachutes from clocks that proved country lore right - with St George's Day over, the dandelions had passed their prime.

My wife's Dyson vacuum earned its keep, the noise driving Bilbo the cat and I to share the peace of the allotments with muddy-wants in wontwiggles and slow worms under rotting compost heaps. There above the trickle-stream, mosquitoes and a midge shroud caught the light of a golden evening to evoke the words penned at Dunster Mill in 1883 by Richard Jeffries as his keen eyes focused on midges above the rippling River Avill:

"They look as if entangled in an inextricable maze, but if you let your eye travel, say to the right, as you would follow the flight of a bird, you find that one side of the current of insects flies up that way, and the other side returns. They go to and fro in regular order, exactly like the fashionable folk in Rotten Row, but the two ranks pass so quickly that looked at both together the vision cannot separate them, they are faster than the impression on the retina."

Meanwhile, there was something else in the allotments air other than nibbling insects. Mania suddenly gripped the cat after she had invited herself inside an open door shed to sniff at mousedom among the spades, trowels, forks, flower pots, stacked deck chairs, grow bags and slug pellets. Coming over all unnecessary she ran around in a demented way with unreliable starey eyes. The dash through the forget-me-nots, and a roll in the freshly raked teddy bed were the warm-up to paw-batting at dumbledores and Orange-tip butterflies, scratching at an emmet-batch and careering through dwarf poly tunnels flattening seedlings of lettuce and rocket.

Then belting up a pear tree to shock a bum-towel into flight she found herself stuck. The realisation of having a reverse gear and that her claws could be used as pitons dawned with wild-eyed wonderment.

The cat's fit of madness became infectious as April showers turned to May drizzle.

In the Old Ship Aground beside Minehead's harbour John Land's crew in their white peaked caps and black and white hooped Breton style shirts began squeezing and pulling their accordions and melodeons to the ritual tune: Der-di-di-dee, der-di-di-dee, der-di-di-dee.

Theirs was a tune that drummers joined, in a town boasting three distinctive hobby horses especially as a small brown affair appeared more pony than horse.

Lop-sided beneath the pub's dart board leaned the real deal – the Traditional Sailors' Hobby Horse. The masked, sackcloth covered, boat-shaped, withy framed, creature decked out in ribbons, ostrich feathers and colour painted 'portholes', was ready for letting loose in the cause of general rumpus. It would be farmed out to a team of muscle-bound, cider-fuelled carriers, each volunteering to individually carry the weight of seventy kilograms on their shoulders for ten to twenty minute stints; men of the calibre of limping, grizzled, John Leach. Once upon a time the hobby horse was stabled in John's Alcombe garage, a place where he tied ribbons while I got a close encounter as a television cameraman. Later I was again to see him through my viewfinder being dragged sozzled from the floor of the Queen's Head on hobby horse finale night, roaring a slurred bawdy sea shanty.

With John having 'passed on', the horse continues to puddle-splash, dance and sashay, whip all and sundry with its hard rope tail, and perform the 'booty' on breast-heaving young women. The lassies are held lengthways in front of the horse as it rises up and down in a bonking motion that symbolises fertility. Amongst the screams and commotion charity buckets for *Help for Heroes* and the Lifeboat are rattled with insistence. However, it wasn't always thus. In its heyday the hobby horse was the main source of loot for those taking part and some bootied girls, it's said, miraculously found themselves pregnant.

Small wonder prurience got the motley ensemble suspended in the 1960s from pitching up in daylight at Dunster Castle during the May celebrations. However after a break of more than forty years and the pill turning fifty, 2010 was to see the old custom dating back to 1792 being revived. Well, this was the date jotted in a notebook by one of John Fownes Luttrell servants as he recorded how the hobby horse was paid the then appreciable sum of five shillings.

The *West Somerset Free Press* did the right by reporting matters. Unfortunately it published the wrong picture. Instead of the Traditional Sailors' Horse, the Original Sailors' Horse was shown to the readership. All hell broke loose in the political minefield. Letters of irritation and anger poured through the editor's letterbox. In his defence the two horses were somewhat alike but it was all about finer points of detail. Phrases like "You should have gone to Specsavers" were in abundance. An apology was demanded even though this was like closing the stable door after the horse had bolted.

How had the mistake happened? I was led to believe that the photographer concerned may have become fooled by a member of the Original's band, a lady of traditional build who, complete with military marching drum, wasn't for arguing with as she beat out thunder with drumsticks.

For Ken Dibble the shenanigans were most important to him; they had always been in his blood: "I've got a natural interest in folk and folk traditions, the hobby horse is one of them, which I've been involved in, one way or another for fifty years. I even used to get official time off school, sanctioned by the headmaster to play the accordion with the hobby horse on May Day."

Indeed, such traditions also course through the blood of Ashley 'Tyger' Hutchings. Founder of *Steeleye Span* and a man with a sense of humour radiating as bright as his musical ability, he had stuck the accordion sound from the Traditional's crew on a CD called *The Mother Of All Morris*, so making it available to the ears of a wider audience by way of *Talking Elephant*. This was nowt to do with pachyderms from Fossett's Circus, but just the name of Ashley's record label.

And there were other windows of opportunity. When the Traditional Sailors' Hobby Horse bowed three times to the cloud veiled sun at six o'clock on May Day morning, with only a few and me to see, it was the signal for Exmoor's May Bank Holiday weekend to begin. Some hoped to cash in, more so if they could get away with charging the seemingly extortionate.

I can report that this was especially true of those preying on the first of the year's grockle throngs with kids to entertain. Smoking clutches in the car queue of panicking drivers belayed the confidence that should human inclination fail machines would take the load. I'm really talking about the steep incline at the entrance to the twenty-fives Deb'n acres of Combe Martin Wildlife and Dinosaur Park at Higher Leigh Manor that causes mechanical mayhem.

Parking attendants could only shrug and repeatedly admit to a folly of the main gate's placement. They were almost embarrassed to confess that the pathways beyond it were merriment only suitable for the kids of feral goats. And they scuttled off as mums and dads argued over whether the ordeal to get in was worth the fifty quid and whether to put their tots in pushchairs or resort to piggybacks. Grans just pursed their lips, deciding to stay put in the car rather than face an alpine challenge.

As it was, and watched by hiding wolves, a sea of human misery sought shelter from the May rain. They crammed under awnings, a great cedar tree or within a faux Egyptian tomb to avoid saturation, helpless as the paths to the animals became slides.

Beside their dark and scummy pool the African penguins looked downcast obviously feeling tummy rumbles. Or was it the collywobbles. About what the pelicans thought I can't comment. The caged lions were constant with their anxious pacing. Lemurs in a pen of celandines were trying to climb a wall to freedom, and the meerkats distracted themselves by playing with rubbish.

One of their kind was separated from the others for its own safety. There was concern that other meerkats might attack it having been handled by humans far too often. Compared to the fear of being devoured by a Tyrannosaurus rex or a water-spitting Dilophosaurus, a few nips and bruises were probably preferable.

Although there was really no need to worry, it's hard to convey to dumb animals the concept of hydraulics and pneumatics built upon a steel framework with a fibreglass body shell coated in painted polyurethane and remote control. But in fairness to the meerkat, Dilophosaurus, or 'two-crested lizard', is one of the earliest known Jurassic theropods and one of the least understood.

And as well as being prominently featured both in the 1993 movie *Jurassic Park* and in the original novel by Michael Crichton, it also appeared in the horror novel *Carnosaur* that was set on a farm in rural England. Written by John Brosnan, under the pseudonym of Harry Adam Knight the book's main character, a local lord, recreated dinosaurs by studying the DNA fragments found in dinosaur fossils, then used them as a basis for restructuring the DNA of chickens. In his dying minutes his lordship imprisoned his wife in a farmhouse where she was devoured alive by a newly hatched Tyrannosaurus. In the meantime the Dilophosaurus killed a member of parliament. Heavy stuff.

With such a gory tale as this, politico Stanley Johnson on the family farm at Nethercote had better count his lucky chickens. When wearing a blue rosette he failed to get elected to a seat across the border in dino-dangerous Deb'n. Then again he always had an adventurous spirit exemplified by riding a worse for wear BSA 500cc twin-cylinder Shooting Star motorcycle four thousand miles from London to Afghanistan, tracing the route of Marco Polo. Now conservation was his thing to the extent of becoming a UN ambassador on migratory species. Exmoor has been the single biggest factor in the making of his caring personality – or so he would have us believe.

A direct descendant of George II on his mother's side and as blond and bouf-fant as his famous son Boris, Stanley speaks lovingly of his home that sits near a photogenic log bridge at the bottom of Room Hill where the Exe boasts both grassy banks and moss-soft trees: "It's the most special valley in England, if not the world. When you have lived somewhere, as I have, for sixty years in the same place, it makes a deep, deep impression. And then, I think, just being away from people most of the time – my father always believed animals were much more important than people, and he was prob-ably right about that."

However, Stanley was not really aware of having an upper-class upbringing as his ex-RAF dad who saw himself as an Exmoor farmer rather than a gentle-man farmer and prone to going to Winsford's Royal Oak and downing his beer along with the rest of them, frequently ended up squiffy – in a respectable sort of way. Lucky for him Ranger his chestnut stallion could find its own way back home down Room Hill's rough track to ford the river and then head through the meadows. As Nethercote struggles to survive finan-cially, so too does my friend Patrick.

Happily, with new electioneering at full throttle an award winning theatre company led by Artistic Director Sandy Maberley also wanted to hear from local Minehead opinion for an international project and this gave Patrick hope. Along with collecting Bakelite, Patrick had a weakness for homing veteran caravans. By chance he came to realise they could generate income.

As a last resort to allow themselves to recuperate after a party at Wyndham House, Lord and Lady Soames chose Patrick's 'Angela', a 1932, aluminium bodied, Bertram Hutchings with leaded windows, green paintwork ticked out in yellow and with red wheel hubs, the picture of prettiness. Inside, her blackcurrant berry patterned wallpaper could be mistaken for whorts and she had a convenient chemical loo. Her ladyship thought her night in Angela "the best night ever". His lordship at six-foot-four thought it a bit short. Patrick presumed he was speaking of the caravan. In future Patrick thought he might be able to charge.

So he had his fingers-crossed that he might earn some pennies from another of his caravans. 'Eggon Ronay', a grey 1956 Willerby Vogue that looked like an egg on wheels, was set to make a public appearance in Minehead's Wellington Square. It was invited to be one of the attractions for a colourful exhibition created by the artists of Bilbrook-based Theatre Mélange endeavouring to generate Minehead nostalgia. The intention was that Patrick's caravan would help focus minds back to when the pier stopping steamers calling at the harbour was demolished and a Brylcream machine could restore a quiff for a penny a squirt.

At the town's station where engines belched steam the theatre company had created an installation entitled *Make do and Mend*. The insides of old railway carriages were decked out with fabrics and kitchen scales, vinyl records and radio sets, even the legs of a mannequin. People came in hundreds to visit and share their memories of Minehead life in the 1950's and early 60's.

The theatre put to good use the reputation it had gained for a style of work fusing image, text and sound to create highly visual, contemporary performance. The two-year collaboration with the University of Exeter also had partners in France and Romania and nearly fifty grand's worth of grant monies had been cobbled together from both home and Europe to answer the question: What do we value about Minehead's past?

The numerous responses covered the years when Butlins replaced the line of jaded beach huts, the old coal ovens in the remaining wall of the town's defunct gas works becoming used as lockups for harbour boatmen and the Quay West landfill rubbish dump became green landscaped. Indeed, for many a local, to see and hear the dump rats 'singing' on a summer evening was the experience of their life.

And there were other highlights before the arrival of the sea wall defences, bulldozers and flats, those dredged from my own childhood memories when I feared the Darkness – the white painted and peeling, concrete and steel, tad ganky, open air Lido swimming pool with its deck chairs, crowds and ten metre high diving stage; the worn out, competitive, crazy golf course offering chipped balls and bent putters for hire; and the cave-like emporium that was Locks Bazaar beside the Regal cinema that sold everything from dusty toys to coconut mats and tin baths.

However, with all the chatter about change both political and otherwise surely the most annoying event was the vanishing of the 'golden' beach. This fell outside the remit of Theatre Mélange. A Minehead stalwart for two decades, Paul Slade, a retiring GP and part-time farmer, remembers the riddle of the sands well. In hindsight the sands weren't as bright as the golden pheasant cock often seen in Allerford Plantation. He thought that quite remarkable due to its type's habit of dropping dead for the sake of it – "too cold, too hot, too quiet, too noisy, any excuse".

Paul's Irnham Lodge doctors practice once boasted its own on-site café complete with alcohol licence and continues to run the medical centre at Butlins. Featured in the '90s BBC series *Doctors Orders* he expressed a whimsy to describe a bunion on the side of a hallux valgus as 'a hurty lump on a twisty toe' and introduced his rambler-chasing gander 'Homicidal Maniac' to the watching world.

As to the events leading up to the missing beach Paul was a credible witness. He was in the majority blaming the very multi-million-pound coastal defence scheme that was supposed to protect the town's asset. The uncharacteristic grinding noise of pebbles being dragged back and thrown forward in a strong swell and receding waves was the first inkling that something was wrong. The sight of children scrabbling among the shingle and mud for any stray sandy grains to build their meagre sandcastles confirmed it.

The problem began in '95 when the town was flooded by fierce storms after they had demolished the old sea defences. Nearly thirteen million pounds were spent by the Environment Agency rebuilding them using huge boulders. They were supposed to reduce the impact of the waves but all they achieved was to affect the tide. Of course there was local fury and narked grockles. Bargefuls of replacement sand amounting to three hundred thousand tonnes had to be ordered at a cost of two and a half million quid.

But it was all worth it. Taking a time out from a Butlins ATP event the band Grizzly Bear gave an impromptu beach concert amidst a small gathering with sand in their shoes. Aided by a single acoustic guitar and with harmonies that lulled and charmed like a Coney Island fairground waltz they sang *Deep Blue Sea,* pushing the bounds of credulity out to the lapping grey waters of the Bristol Channel.

All things considered I'm glad that it's the hobby horses that can provide continuity of sorts. And if the Sailor's horse arrives at the head of the month then Combe Martin's with its black, wooden, small snapping jaws called 'mappers', prances at the tail as Exmoor's hawthorn trees bear a profuseness of snow white blossom.

I stood in the evening light on the green opposite the Pack of Cards pub, that weird and wonderful seventeenth century building of symbolic mathematical pre-metric correctness created by a gaming private school teacher Robert Ley. Built on a plot of land fifty-two feet square the edifice has four floors to represent the number of suits in a pack, thirteen doors on every floor and a similar number of fireplaces to signify the number of cards in a suit, and prior to window tax the panes of window glass added up to the sum of the numbered cards in a pack. However, it wasn't the pub that caused me to gawp.

Their tall conical hats decorated with ribbons, five musket carrying, red coated grenadiers each wearing a pair of red and white striped shorts with skin coloured bum patches bearing two letters, lined themselves up to spell out 'Earl of Rone'. Mop-hatted, white-skirted women in revealing low cut blouses hid their modesty by shawl. A fool held a broom. And dressed up locals, some beating drums, from Combe Martin and the surrounding parishes of Berrynarbor, Trentishoe and Kentisbury swelled the numbers of a not very fierce looking group returning with a masked fugitive wearing sackcloth and a string of ship's biscuits round his neck hunted down in Lady's Wood. The earl had been caught.

Before my eyes the unfortunate soul was pulled from a donkey that he had been ignominiously riding backwards down the longest village street in England, was shot in a volley of musket fire, and then hobby horse bitten. I took a photo of the donkey. It too had biscuits hung around its neck.

To my relief the fool managed to sweep the earl alive only for him to suffer the same torments again. And so the suffering continued as the procession headed towards Raparee cove. With the fool constantly successful with persistent administrations, the grenadiers in the end decided to put pay to the earl once and for all by drowning him in the sea at sunset to much delight and many a cheer.

A young girl seemed quite relieved to be told by her mum that it was a 'stunt double' dummy chucked into the briny and that the 'real' earl was hiding under the hobby horse's skirt to await his 'resurrection' in twelve months time.

Banned in 1837 by the local vicar after he burnt the costumes as punishment for licentiousness and guddling, the custom, that was tied to Ascension Day and which legend says was to do with Hugh O'Neill, Earl of Tyrone, being forced to flee from Ireland in 1607 and getting shipwrecked in the local bay, was revived in 1974. In reality Hugh wasn't shot or drowned but was instead sent to Barnstaple. So really the whole affair was probably just something to wile away some hours, for in truth Combe Martin didn't offer a lot else a do. But it was more of a sociable activity than designing a house based on a deck of cards after school was out.

A day or so later on my way home with a bag of shopping to the relative safety of my blue warped front door I glanced to my left and right and realised with a gulp that I was a target. From out of his tiny pristine cottage Les had emerged on a mission, his wife behind encouraging him forward. "I want to complain about your cat. Two in the morning she was caterwauling and wouldn't stop. I can't believe she made such a racket. You neglecting her? Where were you?"

Taking a tip from politicos not to answer direct questions I was evasive. "She's been a bit sky west and crooked over the past few days. It's bound to wear off, like the election fever."

"Well, just make sure it does."

"No worries." Bilbo was surely just voicing her opinion on the news that Exmoor got squished whorts with a couple of dollops of the custard somehow in the 'cabinet'. For one liking furrows red and green sachets of rabbit this wasn't her cup of tea at all.

And I had my own problem to contend with – still not managing to get that blessed tune 'Der-di-di-dee. Der-di-di-dee' out of my head.

And for those still trying to find out what had become of the donkey Moose-man had spotted on Google Earth standing outside Wivey's White Hart, my photo from Combe Martin proved inconclusive as to whether the legendary beast had found a part-time job. I had to convey that piece of news to the bibblers in the Bearin' Up forthwith.

.

NINETEEN

Deluge and Blisters

"A bear, however hard he tries, grows tubby without exercise."
A.A. Milne, English author, 1882 – 1956.

'Iron Man' Dave was a Musgrove Park Hospital eye registrar of enquiring scientific mind who relished a challenge. I never could tempt him to watch Rex the sheepdog chase cricket balls down at deep fine long leg as he fielded for Wootton Courtenay 2nds nor to snag fish hooks in the branches of sunken trees at Wimbleball or Nutscale reservoirs. Absolutely not. Indeed, he only fished when he had nothing better to do, and that was rarely.

Perhaps this reluctance was due to him being kicked out of the door at the age of six with a rod and hook to catch tiddlers for the family cat. Or maybe it was, as he maintained, the result of coming to Exmoor via an Harare childhood and Oz. Neither Porlock Bay hobbit sharks nor the brown trout and the odd salmon in the 'awesome' River Lyn were up to the challenge of 'Great Whites' in waters that lapped the remote rain forest north of Brisbane. A place where the airstrip for landing a 737 was in a farmer's field, wheelie-bins cordoned off plane engines, the terminal was a corrugated shack to which luggage was delivered by oversized wheelbarrow, the mullet haircut was fashionable along with 'rats-tails' and Pooh Bear was thought of as a stuffed Koala.

Still calling himself Rhodesian just to annoy Zimbabwe's Robert Mugabe, Dave was above all else a sweat fanatic. He had earned the title 'Iron Man' by completing the Dorset-Somerset UK Triathlon: a 2.4 mile swim involving two laps in fog of Sherborne Castle's murky bird-poo-full lake, a 112 miles of frenetic cycle peddling in pretty countryside, and then to conclude, a 26.2 mile full marathon along the A30, through Yeovil, and on up to Montacute House before heading back to the start/finish point in Sherborne.

He was also a chap who had tamed the 'Exmoor Beast'. Not the elusive furry one, but the toughest cyclo sportif in Britain that waggishly goes by the same name. Run every late autumn with a start and finish at Butlins the event offers a choice between two distances – a hundred kilometres or a hundred miles. True to form Dave plumped for the latter and found it a tad arduous.

Within the first ten miles it became clear that with face-stinging, freezing cold rain he was at severe risk of complete exhaustion or hypothermia and had succumbed to walking Dunkery Beacon fearsome gradient in the company of a seventy-one year old, the senior in the throng. By the first feeding station at Simonsbath, where wood burning stoves and hot soup greeted him, Dave swore not to return to Exmoor again until summer came before peddling on to a certificate and commemorative kit bag, displaying the words 'I tamed the beast' - witty words to fuel the legend of fangs and paws with claws in the minds of those who didn't know their handlebars from their bar handled cider taps.

So come June and the first cone-shaped spikes of pale reddish-purple spotted orchids, Dave resplendent in blue lycra torpedo cycle wear removed a fly from between his teeth and remarked that one of the mysteries of life is where flies go in winter. Then he nonchalantly massaged his leg muscles beside his expensive racing bike. That day he had cycled from Taunton to Lynmouth and back passed foxgloves and rose bay willow herb and in doing so had encountered great ups and downs. He achieved the feat almost on the anniversary of the *Pelican* on route from Port Talbot to Highbridge finding herself see-sawing in 1928 on the Gables, the unmarked reef in Minehead Bay. An iron keeled steamship wreck rather than a bird, she lies today starboard side up in the claggy clay off Madbrain Sands.

Thinking of her crew saved by the Minehead lifeboat made my brain cogs turn to another mission of salvation. With a smile I mentioned to Dave that if a large wooden lifeboat pulled by a few horses, aided by repeated shoves from a small collection of humanity, could overcome the extreme gradient offered by Countisbury Hill in a screaming storm, then for someone of his calibre peddling in sunshine, climbing the hill must have been a piece of piddle.

I was referring to the thirteen-mile cross-country ordeal of the *Louisa* on a carriage as wide as barn. Hard to comprehend this also involved going down Porlock Hill, and was a story told by Cyril Walter Hodges, one of the outstanding author-illustrators of his time, in his book *The Overland Launch.*

Ever the purist and preferring to be known as Walter rather than Cyril, he would hurl perfectly good drafts for his latest commission into the bin, starting all over again even after midnight in order to get everything just right. I found him a useful role model - his actions so much more demonstrative than my simple keypad pressing of 'highlight + delete'. His obituary appearing in the *Independent* in 2004 called him "hard-working to the point of perfectionism", and a man of "gentle demeanour and unfailingly sweet temper that brought him universal popularity in addition to well-earned professional respect'". Basically, he was a nice guy.

By also having a reputation as a scholar of the Shakespearean theatre it was understandable Walter was drawn to the drama of a tempest. He told of how in January 1899, in the days before practical inflatables, *Forest Hall*, a three-masted full-rigged ship floundered in the Bristol Channel in a most violent of storms. The *Louisa's* lifeboatmen were unable to put to sea at Lynmouth. Their only chance to save the crew of the *Forest Hall* was to tow the *Louisa* overland to Porlock Weir. In both tasks they were successful.

It had been an incredible achievement. Dave acknowledged it. Despite wobbling on to conquer he admitted to thinking at one point that he was actually going to die on the way up Countisbury Hill. Fifty-three years after the *Forest Hall* incident, and again to the fault of storm, others thought they were going to die at the hill's bottom. Regretfully this time, many did.

Upon the Chains on the 15th August 1952 and out of a sky that had looked summery a weight of nine hundred tonnes of water fell on every acre of land. The Hoar Oak tree, standing as a boundary mark of the ancient Royal Forest, must have felt very sorry for itself. Lynmouth felt even sorrier as ninety million tonnes of water swept down the narrow valley towards it. At about seven o'clock in the evening the West Lyn River broke its banks, took its old course through the centre of the town, joined up with the East Lyn and worked fresh havoc. Due to Lynmouth being a well-known tourist town and suffering heavy loss of life news of the spectacular tended to fill the papers to the exclusion of the carnage in lesser-known places.

Parracombe and Dulverton both looked like the centres of battlefields. At

Exford the torrent rushed across the Green. The first thing the Village Stores knew was that water was spurting through the letterbox. Twenty-two houses were released with axes by men up to their armpits in swirling water. About twenty others had one and a half metres of filthy water in five or six hours.

And at Withypool, a wall of water over three metres high and travelling at great speed down the Barle Valley struck the village. Mr Evan Lock's cow-shed, a dutch barn and ricks containing over twenty tonnes of hay were carried off leaving no trace of their previous existence. Mr Blackmore's garage was washed away and six cars standing in it were covered by water, mud and rubble. Mrs Tresize's little garden looked exactly like a bomb crater. Landacre Bridge was left standing, but the flood went round it and washed the road away. Every fence in the valley between Landacre and Dulverton was flattened out, and every field was covered with stones, boulders, tree-trunks and rubble.

In Lynmouth, Dilys Singleton lost six members of her family, including her grandmother. She recalled: "Mum identified her by this huge wart on her back because she hadn't got no head, or arms, or legs when they found her". She also remembered rumours of planes circling prior to the deluge and survivors telling how the air smelled of sulphur on the afternoon of the floods, and the rain falling so hard it hurt people's faces.

Dave believed in conspiracy theories from earthquake machines to HAARP and was convinced what had happened on Exmoor wasn't an act of God. In Ministry of Defence files papers for the significant period were clearly found to be missing. There were two words that explained things: cloud seeding. Now Dave looked sceptics in the eye, vindicated, saying, 'I told you so' as it's come to light that the disaster came only days after the RAF using adapted gliders made rain-making experiments over southern England coinciding with North Devon experiencing two-hundred-and-fifty times the normal August rainfall.

BBC Radio Four's *Document* programme had revealed 'Operation Cumulus' or as those involved jokingly called it, 'Operation Witch Doctor' and that toasts were drunk to meteorology after 'cloud-seeders' on gliders sprayed salt or chemicals. One of the glider pilots confessed, "The seedsman had said he'd make it rain, and he did. It was not until the BBC news bulletin was read later on that a stony silence fell."

As I keyboard tap, the British Geological Survey are searching for remaining chemical traces in hope of finding conclusive evidence in time for the 50th anniversary of the great deluge.

In the meantime as white spotted red deer calves were born to quiver hidden by long grass and bracken fronds, Dave, fancying a stroll, had an appointment of a totally different nature to keep – the Perambulation. Taking place annually for over seven and a quarter centuries in the paradise of blood-sucking, skin-burrowing ticks it was Exmoor's longest one-day walking event. And due in part to early effects of climate change the ticks were on the increase creating anxiety for farmers. Tick-borne diseases such as louping ill and red water fever affect both sheep and cattle. Yes, there was local immunity but introductions were stressful. Also, the 'Perambulators' must have found it disconcerting to know that cases of Lyme disease were on the up, however, they seemed undeterred with antibiotics so easy to come by. Doctors, too, were about to become close to hand.

Dave had heard of the mega stomp through a madly effusive hospital nurse. She was one of a horde of two hundred yompers from around the country coming together every June to tramp thirty-one miles around the boundary of the old Royal Forest where John Knight's stone walls provide nesting crannies for wheatears, those invaluable destroyers of pests.

In principle the Perambulation sounded easy - most of the route lay over open moorland upon which molinia grass, cotton grasses, tussock grass and deergrass flourished, a small amount of road walking and just three watercourses to cross before finishing back at Pinkery. And there was an order to it: The Saddle Gate – Brendon Two Gates – Black Barrow – Alderman's Barrow – Picked Stones Lane.

The lane was the halfway point. Picked Stones Farm is still referred to by locals as 'Picket Stones'. Since it lay on the forest boundary some large stones set on end probably served as pickets or boundaries here. From the lane it was on to White Post, then across Sherdon Water to Two Barrows on the ridge between Hangley Cleave and Fyldon Common, from whence it was back again to Pinkery via Moles Chamber and the Edgerley Stone.

For Dave it was a new challenge. Yes, there would still be flies, but it was a particularly attractive proposition as he could snoop at an Exmoor never seen from his cycle saddle and not normally accessible to the public riff-raff. Wanting to share the experience he cast around for a partner to march with. And as luck would have it he found one in Li, a diminutive Chinese doctor from Cardiology. That year there would be two unregistered participants among those with cagoules, hiking sticks, plastic map holders, compasses and rucksacks full of sandwiches, drinks and mint cake.

Choosing my words carefully I told Dave that Badgworthy Cottage, on the route somewhere beyond Brendon Two Gates, was home to Jack Little, perhaps the best of all Exmoor shepherds, and sported a roof with 'Teas' painted across the slates. "Ideal, I'll just carry my wallet," said Dave.

Unable to find the start that was in the yard of Pinkery's Outdoor Education Centre, Dave was late. Li popping up on a putt-putt motorcycle with knapsack and hiking boots was even later. Both had missed the off and both were without a map or a compass. They were scowled at by some officials. And they scowled even more when Dave and Li said they didn't know that they had to register or pay an entry fee to the Exmoor Youth Association.

Dave asked if there was any good reason why either he or Li couldn't just join in.

"What if you get lost?" asked an official, sensibly.

"Get lost? How can we?" Dave responded. "Here there are houses, walls and roads. You should try going from Woy Woy to Woop Woop in the Australian bush."

"Have either of you got any of these things with you?" asked the official pointing out at a list that included: Warm sweater, spare socks and hand towel, survival bag/blanket capable of enclosing the whole body, torch with efficient bulb and batteries, waterproof hat, coat and trousers, sun hat or similar.

Dave adjusted his gun-silver Oakley sport sunglasses. "No."

"Well, on your heads be it. Head out north-west. After two hundred paces turn right over the hill and try and catch up. And don't go scaling a fence where there's a gate. Don't fail to re-fasten a gate. Oh, and if you're serious don't go taking any short cuts, you're going to be walking on private land!" The official's voice trailed away.

Before too long they caught the tail passing Wood Barrow and from then on followed anyone in front over Thorn Hill and across the high moor passed the

Hoar Oak tree to Brendon Two Gates.

There are no gates at Brendon Two Gates now, just a cattle grid. Once, though, two gates hung from a single post and opened in opposite directions, and with Exmoor at its most ingenious best, so no matter which way the wind blew it would blow one gate shut. Business minded young whippersnappers used to collect pennies from riders by opening the gates for them. On the day of the perambulation when Dave got there he apparently needed to spend one.

After a preoccupied zip-tug, had Dave looked to his right he couldn't have missed noticing Lanacombe where Exmoor's last domestic fuel cuttings of peat were made in 2007, and where Sante Lafuente achieved one thousand five-hundred spits on a good day. Sante, a peat-digger, the designer of his own spade and an extreme 'furriner', came to England in May 1937 as a fourteen-year-old refugee with five thousand others aboard the *Havana* to escape the Spanish Civil War Fascist attacks on his home in San Sebastian.

Aged sixty-nine, Sante was interviewed for the HTV series *Secrets of the Moor* in which he explained his trade: 'Most peat digging goes on in spring because you need dry, fine, windy weather and rain is terrible. You take off the top layer, place it carefully on a dug bed so that it will grow again. You dig out the spits and lay them out. They take ten days to dry, then you turn them over. After another week they will be bone hard, just like coal, and very good for your fire.' The deeper the beds the blacker was the peat that tended to break up into lumps when being dried. Such lumps were known as 'biddocks'. Bagged up separately, they were highly prized for giving out exceptional heat.

In the same year as Exmoor's peat digging died so also did Victor Bonham-Carter considered by some as one of the greatest authorities on the Exmoor scene. For me he had been a bit of a hero for another reason. Writing in the *Independent* obituaries Mark Le Fanu opined that Victor's "two-volume Authors by Profession (1978-84) is the most comprehensive history ever written of the evolution of authorship as a business. In elegant prose, laced with anecdotes, it traces the fragile economics of surviving as a writer, the development of copyright and the perennially tricky - and therefore fascinating - nature of relations between authors and publishers."

He was part of the 28-year campaign to secure Public Lending Right, under which authors receive a small payment each time one of their books is borrowed from a public library. His years of speaking engagements and tireless lobbying culminated in legislation in 1979 and the annual payments made to authors since 1984.

Twenty years ago whilst living at Milverton, Victor had written his pièce de rèsistance *The Essence of Exmoor*. However, when he wrote this book it's unlikely that he considered that that essence might be either gorse or heather.

Vivian had come from Norfolk to volunteer an interview for a documentary about living alternative lifestyles. For reasons of penury I had found myself involved. At Landacre Bridge, weighed down by an impressive pendant, and squinting beneath a wide brimmed blue cloth hat as the sun played peek-a-boo behind clouds, Vivian talked to camera about making flower essences to help her believers reconnect with nature.

With her she had a box containing a score of tiny bottles each containing trace dilutions of this and that. Selecting one labelled 'Heather' she held it to the lens, saying: "If you feel lonely heather will help you find companionship inside." I thought to put some drops into the glass tank of my home alone goldfish before forcing myself to concentrate on the job in hand.

"Through the ills of the world we have become disconnected from our true roots," she preached. "With flower essences your own body is your laboratory. I see essences as soul food, feeding us inside on the emotional level, the mental level and the spiritual level. When you feed the soul miraculous things can happen."

"Oh look at that colour!" she breathed, suddenly distracted by some gorse in bloom beside her. "I can feel the heat warming my soul. It fills me with a golden smile and smells like vanilla-coconut. It takes me straight to my sun tan lotion and to a lovely tropical beach. Gorse is a remedy for hopelessness when people have become half dead with life."

Suppressing a tut, I turned and looked wistfully upstream thinking not of the twelve-foot high wave that once rushed over where we stood engulfing all that was in its path but of a true countrywoman of small size yet giant inner strength who would have undoubtedly given Vivian's fay philosophies short thrift.

On a bumpy track above where the Barle and Sherdon Water join I had pushed the red button to record both Hope Bourne narrating her book *Wild Harvest* and a howling gale to tape. The two of us were huddled inside my wind-buffeted car within sight of her beloved Ferny Ball where she lived for years in a caravan in the garden of a fire-destroyed farmhouse. She had lived by shooting meals, cooking fry-ups and seven-mile weekly treks to Withypool to buy a loaf of bread. Hope loathed being 'indoors', always had. She found it claustrophobic. Now, her head scarf-wrapped, her face as wrinkled as a walnut, a studio would have been a greater Hell than the sheltered housing the local council had encouraged her to move to in Withypool. To her being in car was a concession just so long as she could see 'home'. Anyway, from my point of view where we sat added 'atmosphere'.

Taking a breather from the pages she said: "There are many areas of beauty and many sorts of beauty, natural and man-made, but the thing that matters here is what is left of the wilderness. It's something I think that we need, we need our roots and our roots are not in civilisation."

"So, our border patrols of weasels needed to be extra vigilant of meddlers?" I asked.

"Oh yes," she laughed, "they do."

The Perambulation took Dave and Li eleven hours to complete and officials were as surprised to see them finish as see them start. However, neither Dave nor Li received a cloth badge or a Finisher's Certificate. Their only reward was the satisfaction of achievement and blistered ulcerated feet.

Li was the first to say that she had had good fun, adding: "That was Exmoor's true heart. Although, given its sogginess it's one I would diagnose as having cardiomyopathy." As I cringed at a comment a bit near the bone, both she and Dave concurred that the moor needed intensive care. I agreed, too, supposing that by declaring Exmoor a National Park what is left of its wilderness character will be preserved.

"There were no cottage selling teas," grumbled Dave. I confessed that Badgworthy Cottage had done so in the late nineteenth century but fell victim to wartime military training. What Dave said then is unrepeatable. Undaunted I went on to say that the cottage wasn't the only casualty. Ken Baker's Gran died in her forties. Ten years before, a live bullet in the peat turf on fire went off when she was cooking. It shattered the saucepan and pieces went into her head making her turn insane.

Having collected his thoughts, Dave asked what happened to Dick Little.

"Um, I think he went to live at the cottage at Wheal Eliza. Now that's rubble, too." I said.

"Strewth," said Dave, "Spending so much time with sheep must have made neglectful of home."

It began to rain and through the pitter-patter came the sound of a distant plane.

TWENTY

Endpiece

*"Buzzards may soar in the clouds, but weasels never
get sucked into jet engines."*

Anon.

Found east of Frome in a field of buttercups and squatted in by a non-mechanically minded assortment of wildlife of insects, spiders, birds and rodents was a 1960s mobile cinema bus that had once toured the nations factories. The futuristic steel framed, perspex-glazed dome above the cab that had housed the remote control projection equipment was green with algae, complimenting nicely the bus's overall colour.

The animals thought the whole caboodle very useful and, with gearbox and gear stick having been nicked, the bus certainly didn't seem inclined to go anywhere any more. KJU 267E had literally been put out to pasture. It was the last remaining of seven custom mobile cinema units built by the Ministry of Technology to promote modern production techniques to British industry.

Then in October 2003 the squatters suddenly became evicted. An enterprising couple Rob Howell and Nancy-Rose Mills had decided to become itinerant movie entrepreneurs and the bus was their means of achieving that aspiration. They hitched the bus a lift on a HGV low load and the threesome embarked upon a new life in North Devon aided by Lottery funds.

Then come spring 2010, oh happy joyfulness. The movie bus, fully and lovingly restored in fine white and blue livery, and under its own volition, hit the roads of Exmoor in fine fettle. And news of the resurrection made it the star of a short BBC *Inside Out* documentary. Aboard the vintage bus were comfy seats for punters, a screen, digital projection equipment and suitable films provided by the South West Film and TV Archive. Locals from you name it could have the opportunity once more to relive events like the Lynmouth flood disaster or see for themselves grainy images of the furry variety of Exmoor Beast. This was heritage on wheels that to me seemed very important given the subjective nature of the written word.

Worryingly with such excitements going on in the wider world things have a habit of happening in Wivey without me noticing. But safe to say, in the *Larder* Lois looked flustered. "I'm all hot and bothered after the delivery," she said with heavy breathing.

"I don't know what to make of that," I said paying for my shallots. "Should you be at work?"

"Oh, you've got much more important things to think about."

She was right, of course. Better that than start to gossip when the crates of fresh autumn vegetables, bags of lentils, and boxed jars of preserves stacked beside two sacks of teddies were clear for all to see.

Had I not known better I might have thought my cat hadn't moved from the cushion onto which she had eased herself when I first pondered on the Bright Ember's directive on sub-culture. It had been almost a year since I had eaten curried beetroot and chatted with Chaggi in the hills of Nilgiris and vowed to reacquaint myself with Exmoor. And I had. Although the starlings seemed to gossip that in so doing I merrily put back the kilos of Indian loss.

Yet, on my excursions I had discovered some other rumours of change had been nothing other than stories taller than the giant reedmace of Dunster's brackish marsh. With its heads resembling mangy-sheep suffering from alopecia, it hid the view of Conygar Tower from the beach huts by the Horn, as did the billowed smoke of steam trains. And I could assure myself that despite a few things here and there reflecting the nature of our modern times, I generally found Exmoor cared for and in reasonably rude health.

But there was a caveat.

While sparrowhawks with airborne pirouettes snatch blackbird and thrush at Robbers Bridge, sadly there had been other losses in past years like the black grouse and the hamlet of Clicket. And after Tesco's ruthlessly wooed and dumped them, Tower Farms, producers of beloved local cheese and cream, had suffered irreversible down-come. Yet folk just tut and shrug and carry on doing what they were doing when told the humble hornet robber fly and the unexceptional ballerina waxcap fungus are readying for the off. Perhaps it should be banged in with a mallet that it's in such microcosms of existence as these that change insidiously begins.

Both Bury's veteran oak tree and the Hoar Oak tree were potentially endangered, as indeed were all of Exmoor's English oaks. A mysterious blight was attacking quercus robur up and down the length of Britain - a news story that seemed to have come and gone.

So from somewhere upon Exmoor we may need to find volunteer help to address the problem. Thinking this, I was reminded of Jean Giano's most lovely and poignant of little books *The Man who Planted Trees* about the imaginary, yet wholly believable shepherd Elzeard Bouffier who spent his working life planting acorns while tending his sheep. Time then for an aspiring Jack Little to step forward though only of course with the blessing of the National Park.

However, on the bright side there was still an abundance of edible wonderfulness out there in the year's new cycle of mists, chill air, gossamer webs and shortening days of brown, copper and gold. As buzzards vouched for bunnies, pink-twinks would soon begin hunting for beechmast. And with a little bit of sun and a little bit of wet it was picking season for me again - the harvest of hedgerow, mossy bank and fruitful moor.

Scrabbling under the passenger seat of the car for some precious, basket escaping, boletus ceps and some rogue blackberries I rediscovered Frederick Snell's *Book of Exmoor*. It was covered in welly boot mud. I had completely forgotten about the blessed thing recommended to me many months previously by the Bright Ember and presumed that it must have slid off the back seat on some occasion when I had had to brake suddenly for the regulars of fezzie, badger or tractor. Or maybe it happened with one of those near disasters like the hind bolting out of trees on Cloutsham Ball or the little white-haired lady driving her Range Rover like a pipistrelle out of hell near Molland.

The book find though had come too late for any further Exmoor wandering for the time being. Cocooned behind the warped blue front door there were other important things to do like giving my wife a hug and ordering the winter store of logs from Mr Billinger to ensure the daddygranfers and frogs had shelter and the cat had hearthrug warmth.

And with the ceps awaiting a saddle of rabbit and blackberries their crumble, I stirred sugar into the blue syrup that bubbled in the pan. I absorbed myself in making whortleberry jam, the first pots of the season from the tiny delights gathered before Exmoor's grazing red deer got to them first. Eating whorts it was rumoured can reverse memory loss. Second World War pilots allegedly swore by them having a beneficial effect on night vision. So I thought to persevere in giving whorts a try, if only to find things forgotten in the Darkness.

Ask any yellow-toothed, border patrol Aksmoar weasel on stag duty. The Emperor was still bolving somewhere out there beneath geminid showers, jet trails and falling oak leaves. But that's not to say I wouldn't be squeezing my toothpaste tube to vent the emotion of deep held anxiety. When it came to Exmoor amour I treasured the things that were most dear.

Exmoor Verbage

Aarr: Yes
Aggy: Gather eggs as in "I be gwain aggy."
Alice: Ulcer, so be careful when christening your daughter
Aksmoar: Exmoor
All to lippets: Fallen to pieces
Amper: Pimple
Ann Summer: More handsome, and nothing to do with sex aids

Ballyrag: To scold, tell off especially with foul language
Baven: Faggot of unprepared twigs and branches
Begrumpled: Offended
Benapt: Left high and dry by the tide
Betwaddled: Confused
Bibber: Shiver
Bibbler: One who enjoys a pint or two
Biddle: Beetle
Bim-boms: Church bells
Bivver: Shiver
Boggler: A horse given to stumbling, but not falling.
Bucket-and-chuck-it: The outdoor loo.
Bull-beggar: Hobgoblin
Bum-towel: Long-Tailed Tit.

Caddle: Confusion, muddle
Cage of teeth: A large number, many
Chapper: Fellow, chap
Chim-cham: Undecided, vague talk
Clinkerbell: Icicle
Cleeve: Steep slope
Colley: Blackbird
Come-by-chance: Illegitimate
Clitter-to-clatter: Derisive description of woman 'going-on' about a particular thing

Crousty: Ill-tempered

Dabster: Expert
Daddicky: Rotten
Daddygranfer: Woodlouse
Daug-tuy'urd: Knackered
Dazzy-snoo: Definitely
Deb'n: Devon
Dewbit: Breakfast
Dimpsey: Half lit, at twilight or dusk
Dinnum: Didn't they
Dirsh: Thrush
Dish-washer: Grey wagtail
Down-come: A fall in income.
Draffit: Vessel in which to collect pig swill
Drang: Alleyway
Driggle-Draggle: In a slovenly manner applied to a woman's dress.
Drowner: Employed to cut osiers in the dykes of Sedgemoor
Drowning the Miller: Pouring too much water to make the tea too weak
Dumbledore: Bumble bee

Emmets: Tourists in large numbers
Emmet-batch: An ant-hill
Evet: A lizard

Fairy: A weasel
Farty: Forty
Fezzie: Pheasant
Fuz-pig: Hedgehog

Gallybeggar: Bugbear, hobgoblin
Ganny-cock's Snob: The long membranous appendage at the cock-turkey's beak
Gawk: Stare
Git: Gate – So don't be alarmed if anyone says they're off to hang one.
Goozegogs: Gooseberries
Grockle: Tourist
Grockle shells: Caravans
Guddler: A heavy alcoholic drinker

Gulch: Swallow fast
Gurt, girt: Great

Hellier: Roof tiler
Hoon: Throw with vigour
Horse-stinger: A dragonfly
Hunky punks: Gargoyle

Jack-o-lanterns: Will-o-the-wisps, the souls of unbaptized children

Kern: Turn from blossom to fruit

Larn: Teach

Lilyhangers: Cow's teats

Maized: Mad, insane
Mower: Moor
Muddy Want: Mole
Mugglin: Struggling

Narry: Narrow
Nestle tripe: Runt, especially of pigs
Nottled: Really cold

Oaks: Club suit in a card pack. Oak be trumps in Horner Wood / There they
    growed and there they stood.

Pack and fardel: Bag and baggage
Pew Moanier: Pneumonia
Pink-twink: Chaffinch
Pixie led: Simple minded, crazed
Praper: Excellent
Puggle 'eaded: Drunk. Cider drinkers can often be recognised by their rosy
    faces and inability to articulate. They are then considered puggle 'eaded

Quaddle: Waddle
Queechy: Sickly

Quats: Sit down suddenly. A stag 'quatted' when he took a great leap sideways and flattened himself to the earth in a piece of bracken

Rampin: Raving mad
Rain-pie: Woodpecker
Ruckles: Peat stacks

Scollared: Taught
Smeech: Smoky smelling
Snap-jack: Stitch-wort
Splat: Small plot of land
Sprunch: Copulate
Spypost: Signpost
Squinch: Nook
Stare-basin: Glow-worm
Suant: Smoothness, evenness, ease in turning or moving
Swing-swang: Rope

Tarble: Terrible
Teddy: Potato
Teetsy-totsy: Cowslip
Thick-wet: Combination of mist-rain-fog-and-drizzle
Tinkerments: A lot of useless gadgets.
Titty-todger: Wren

Unket: Uncanny

Viddy: Right

Wevet: A spider's web
Whister-twister: A smart blow on the side of the head
Wopse: Wasp
Wontwiggle: A mole tunnel

Yes: An earthworm

Zummat: Something
Zummerzet: Somerset